Sacred Light

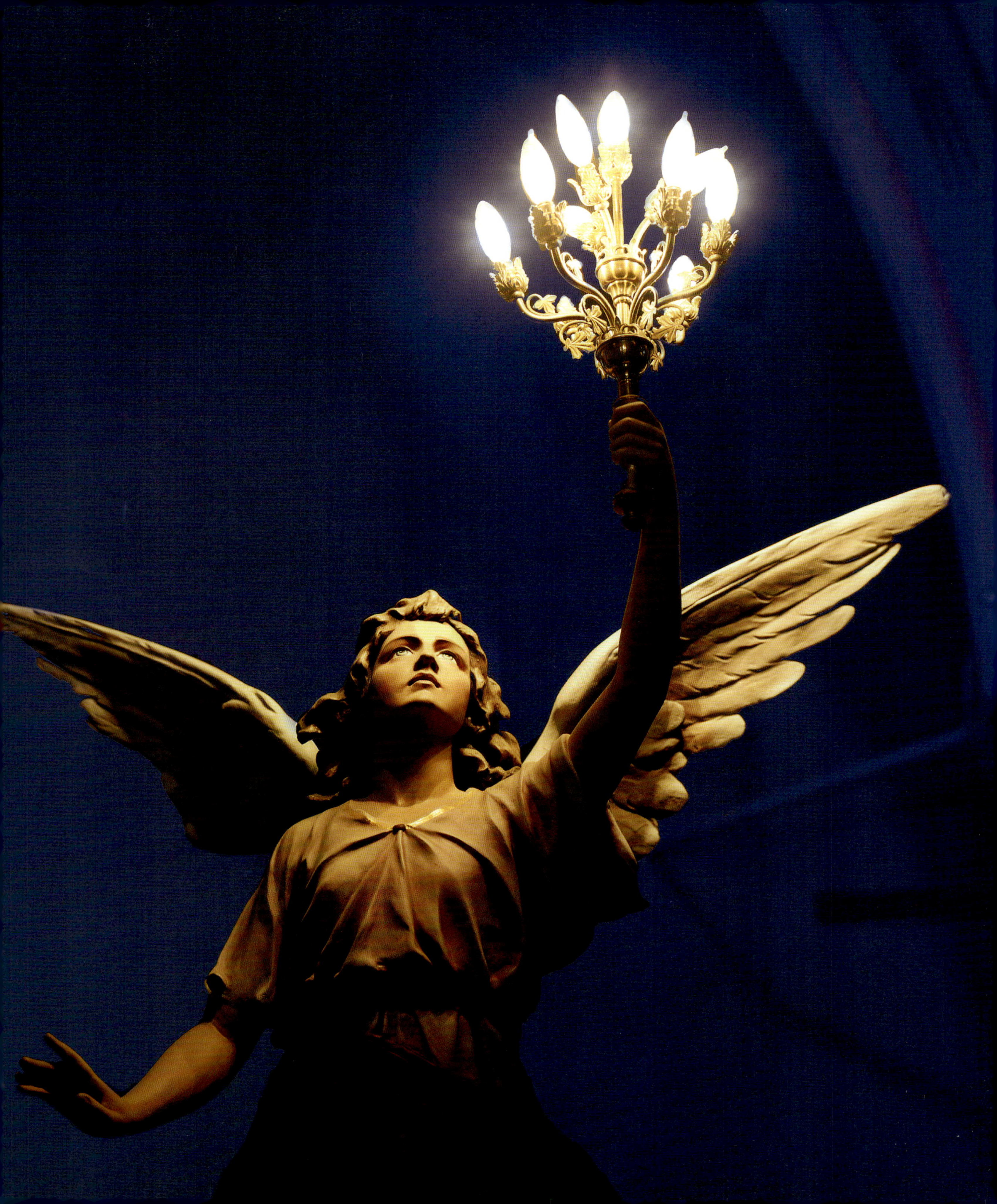

Sacred Light

Holy Places in Louisiana

A. J. MEEK

Essay by Marchita B. Mauck

UNIVERSITY PRESS OF MISSISSIPPI JACKSON

To Otis B. Wheeler

Humanitarian, scholar, photographer, and friend

www.upress.state.ms.us

The University Press of Mississippi is a member of the Association of American University Presses.

Name of printing company: Tien Wah Press (Pte) Limited
Plant location: Singapore

First printing 2010
Library of Congress Cataloging-in-Publication Data

Meek, A. J.
Sacred light : holy places in Louisiana / A.J. Meek ; essay by Marchita B. Mauck.
p. cm.
Includes bibliographical references.
ISBN 978-1-60473-741-7 (cloth : alk. paper) — ISBN 978-1-60473-742-4 (ebook)
1. Church buildings—Louisiana—Pictorial works. 2. Synagogues—Louisiana—Pictorial works.
3. Light in architecture—Pictorial works. I. Mauck, Marchita B. II. Title.
NA5230.L8M44 2010
726.509763—dc22   2010004445
British Library Cataloging-in-Publication Data available

PHOTOGRAPHER'S COMMENTS

In his essay "A Calling of Voices," from his book *The Hungering Dark*, the theologian Frederick Buechner wrote of an aesthetic experience he witnessed on a lonely windswept beach:

. . . you are walking along an empty beach toward the end of the day, and there is a gray wind blowing, and a seagull with a mussel shell in its beak flaps up and up, and then lets the shell drop to the rocks below, and there is something so wild and brave and beautiful about it that you have to write it into a poem or paint it into a picture or sing it into a song; or if you are no good at any of these, you have to live out at least the rest of that day in a way that is somehow true to the little scrap of wonder that you have seen.[1]

From the time I read these words I realized that I had a sacred purpose in life—a ministry—through the medium of photography. My images could bring a little bit of light, inspiration, and sometimes humor into a torn and battered world.

Another artist, London bookseller and photographer Frederick H. Evans (1853–1943), spent his career in relentless search for splendor. He made fine art photographs of many English cathedrals and printed them on platinum paper. He regarded those and French châteaus as places of great beauty and the proper subject matter for his craft. For a photographic artist during the time, the search for beauty needed no explanation. Because the medium was young, the term "documentary"[2] was not yet apropos for photographers engaged in camera vision.

Mid-twentieth-century historians and practitioners widely accepted three major styles of photography—pictorial, documentary, and metaphor or equivalents. Alfred Stieglitz (1864–1946) was often referred to as the father of modern photography, for he cultivated separate bodies of work in each of the categories. Debatably the equivalents of clouds became the most important.

In the article "How I Came to Photograph the Clouds," Stieglitz wrote, ". . . clouds were there for everyone—no tax as yet on them—free."[3] The cloud series (1925–1931), made at his family's summer home in upstate New York's Lake George, suited his style. On a hill, he used a handheld 4 x 5 Graflex camera fitted with a long cardboard snoot to darken the light in order to see the image clearly on the camera's focusing screen. The arrangement allowed him an angle directly overhead to the sky without painfully bending his back, as most eye-level viewfinder cameras would require. Though many of the pictures served as purely documentary images used in schooling meteorologists at the time, Stieglitz thought the images functioned principally on an emotional level.

Considered by some to be one of the greatest composers of the twentieth century, violinist Ernest Bloch (1880–1959), on viewing the pictures, compared the visual works to music. Stieglitz never said they were equivalent to music but found satisfaction in letting each person experience whatever individual emotional response was appropriate. He wrote in the same article "that unless one has *eyes* and *sees*, they won't be seen."[4]

In English pubs I have visited, one can sense centuries of interesting conversation and merriment stuck in the very fabric of each brick and wooden table. Likewise, in the sanctuaries of churches and synagogues, the vibrations of songs, prayers, and comforting words offered over time stick like a coat of tacky damp varnish on the pews and in the crevices of holy places. How many generations have asked for healing for themselves, their children, or their aging parents? How many have found answers to their prayers there? How many shouts of joy can one perceive in the sacred silence? How many friendly handshakes? How many hugs? If you listen you can imagine hearing the hushed vibrations and murmured confessions that relieve a soul's burdens.

A photographer's field experience is undeniably richly filled with memorable experiences. In Europe, during the week, curious tourists often fill places of worship to capacity. In the United States, I found most sanctuaries empty except on Sunday or during a wedding or funeral.

One place in particular is Saint Michael's Catholic Church in Convent, the first church I photographed for this project on sacred light. At the door, a statue of the Archangel Michael met me. The armed figure rested his body on the handle of a wicked, twisting sword blade. Inside, I noticed a man sweeping and carrying a trash can. I thought he was the janitor and then realized he was a Jesuit priest with the appearance of an everyday workman. Another time, an excited student assistant with the camera and a tripod over his shoulder ran up the aisle to set up a picture, exclaiming, "This is the money shot!" More emotional was our panic as we heard the sound of the maintenance crew locking the door, unaware that we were inside making photographs.

Just when I felt the project was nearing completion, Hurricane Katrina ripped the Gulf Coast apart on August 29, 2005. It hit New Orleans especially hard with flooding that caused devastating damage to both people and property. The loss of home and displacement of community were heart-wrenching. Less than a month later, Hurricane Rita slashed into nearby Cameron Parish and Lake Charles.

When the dawn shone its light on Katrina's ravages, many south Louisiana residents began repairing damages and removing debris without knowing the storm had compromised the New Orleans levees and without even suspecting the horror soon to flood the Crescent City.

The storm left tens of thousands stranded in attics, on rooftops, in ill-prepared and storm-damaged facilities, and on the few patches of high pavement. Their suffering flooded New Orleans as surely as the relentless water. Many of the anguished refused rescue until their beloved pets could accompany them.

Filmed images of the misery filled American newspapers and television and exposed the shame of the ill-prepared response to the world.

I had been photographing the interiors of churches and synagogues for seven years prior to Katrina. This was the contrast, the shadow side I was looking for. However, I could not bring myself to make photographs in New Orleans for more than a year after the storm. There had been too much pain, too many photographs of the damage.

It took courage for me to enter the city for the first time after the hurricane. Then, to hear the stories of people who had lost their communities took even more courage. People needed to tell their stories and needed others to listen as part of the healing process.

More than six feet of filthy water completely devastated Beth Israel Synagogue on Canal Street. Congregants risked wading through dangerous, fetid water to rescue the sacred Torah scrolls. With desperate hope, they set sodden prayer shawls and historic photographs in the air to dry, but the help came too late for the ruined artifacts.

The wind ripped a section of the roof from one of St. Alphonsus Catholic Church's[5] towers and carried it a few blocks away. It landed with its cross, which had adorned the building's apex, buried headfirst in the ground. The gash in the roof exposed the church's interior to Katrina's merciless rains.

And, I heard stories of further desecration—stories about thieves who looted the sacred spaces, taking priceless artifacts, which they sold for personal gain.

Photographing in New Orleans, driving by the damaged structures and sacred buildings leaves a definite scar on the psyche. Years later, it still is heartbreaking to hear the stories of too many congregations now dispersed in Katrina's diaspora and the remaining few determined to rebuild. Most poignant is that people want their sacred spaces restored, but some churches and synagogues have only five or six members of their congregations remaining.

Photographs jog the memory of personal history, such as remembrances of weddings and funerals. Losing photographs—the visual records of personal history—is a uniquely painful violation. It is often what grieves people the most after the initial shock of such devastation subsides. They can fix or rebuild structures. Treasured photographs are irreplaceable.

I believe in the determination of the human spirit to build community and restore order.

Ultimately, the reason I photograph these places is that being inside offers a quiet refuge from chaos and confusion. It is a search for beauty, and I can make photographs in peace. That is reason enough.

For some, a technical explanation is deemed both important and interesting. I use a 4 x 5 wooden field camera on a tripod. I load my holders with daylight film and have them processed at a professional color lab. From that point everything is digitized. The transparency is scanned, electronically cleaned, and eventually printed with the use of archival inks and museum-quality paper.

The photographs are usually not manipulated in any fashion. The often-strange color is the way I found it, with the light coming from the color of stained-glass windows or the mixture of daylight and unfiltered tungsten balance. Occasionally the photograph was filtered to convert daylight to a 3400 K rather than a 3200 K incandescent light source for a slightly cooler result.

Not always obvious in some of the photographs are the long exposures, several seconds to, in some instances, several minutes in duration. Astronomers making deep space photographs realize that light collects through the lens and onto the film, making a dark sky seem full of stars. Likewise, a dark interior, given enough time, will result in the same effect.

I especially wish to thank Marchita Mauck for hours of consultation and advice; Lee Davis, my preliminary editor; Gillian Sims, technical expertise; at the University Press of Mississippi, Craig Gill, assistant director and editor-in-chief, for his support of this project, and John Langston, assistant director and art director; Otis B. Wheeler (1921–2008), whose books on churches have been inspiring; Zack Godshall, a talented filmmaker; and Tom Abel, a former monk and father of five, the latter two for assisting, with hard work, hours of riding, listening to my general complaints, pontificating on photography theories, and helping make this project happen.

A. J. Meek

Notes

1. Frederick Buechner, "A Calling of Voices," in *The Hungering Dark* (San Francisco: Harper and Row, 1969), 26.

2. "Documentary" photography was possibly first attributed to Dorothea Lange (1895–1965) in an article on documentary photography published in *A Pageant of Photography* (San Francisco: Crocker-Union, 1940), 28. Reprinted in Nathan Lyons, ed., *Photographers on Photography: A Critical Anthology* (Englewood Cliffs, NJ: Prentice-Hall, Inc., in collaboration with the George Eastman House, New York, New York, 1966), 67. In some regards, all photography, no matter how abstract, is rooted in the documentary style on one level or another.

3. First published in *The Amateur Photographer & Photography*, vol. 56, no. 1819: 225. Reprinted in Lyons, ed., *Photographers on Photography: A Critical Anthology*, 110.

4. Ibid.

5. It is now a struggling community center.

HOUSES OF WORSHIP: CONTEMPORARY PARABLES

A passage in the Hebrew Bible recounts the story of Jacob's dream (Genesis 28:11–19). On a journey to Haran, Jacob stops for the night, places a stone under his head, and falls asleep. While asleep he has a vision of a ladder anchored on the ground but reaching all the way into heaven. Angels (God's messengers) are ascending and descending the ladder. The Lord speaks to Jacob and promises him that he shall have the lands upon which he sleeps, and that he and his descendents shall be as numerous as the motes of dust on the earth, spreading throughout the world, becoming a blessing to all the earth. Awaking from this astonishing dream, Jacob declares that "Surely the Lord is in this place . . . This is none other than the house of God, and this is the gate of heaven." He names the place Bethel, the "house of God." Jacob took the stone that he had put under his head, set it up as a memorial, and poured oil over it.

Jacob felt the need to commemorate his encounter with God by anointing a memorial stone in consecration of the *locus,* to forever mark the place where heaven touched earth. Houses of worship in our own day are likewise places consecrated by and for encounters with the divine. Believers come to these houses of God expecting to discover their own place in the ongoing story of God's epiphany and interaction with people.

Just as in Jacob's day, the faithful discover that memories of the transforming, life-altering moments that they experience forever consecrate these places as holy.

People's lives are often altered by words from holy texts that they hear in a new way. Or they bond with intentional communities to accomplish great deeds of compassion or love. For some the ancient cadences of recited creeds or the Lord's Prayer, or Shabbat Psalmody, or the melodies and texts of familiar hymnody provide grounding in a world seemingly gone awry. Eucharistic prayers from the first century of Christianity recall the redemptive deeds of a God of unconditional love whose story yet has no end. Every community's place of worship over time becomes spirit soaked with tears of grief and joy that are the fabric of the human/divine journey. Conversions, baptisms, and first communions mark the stirrings of faith and incorporation into the community. Blessings are invoked upon countless couples who make vows of "love until death" as they wed in hope and faith. And when the faithful's earthly pilgrimage is completed, in funeral rites mourners commend the spirits of their loved ones to the Creator who first breathed life into them. Lives are consecrated to God in ministry, and maturation rites are celebrated for the young in community rites of confirmations and bar and bat mitzvahs. Christians are fed at the Eucharistic table that they might become as Christ beyond the doors of the church. Communities of faith gather in times of catastrophe to collectively invoke the help and strength of God to persevere through great difficulties, or to express gratitude for blessings received.

When a place of worship's familiar presence is destroyed by natural disaster, or threatened by the merging of communities, or even by renovation plans, anxiety often overwhelms people. It is fascinating that when asked what they might miss most, many will begin by saying, "This is the place . . . this is the place where I made my first communion, or I was married, or my children were baptized, or where my family prayed when I was a child and where we held my grandparents' funerals. This is the place I loved to come to as a child. I remember the smell of beeswax candles, the feel of worn hardback hymnals, the shards of color saturating the backs of pews or floors as sunlight streams through stained-glass windows." Only then will they speak of the altar or sanctuary furniture, or statues, or beautiful stained-glass windows. Because people's stories are anchored in this place, because the transitions of their lives are blessed and consecrated in this place, this place is holy. The visual vocabulary of "holy place" as it has evolved over time blends piety, popular perceptions of beauty and dignity, some iconic elements of architecture traditionally associated with houses of worship, and an intangible yet pervasive sense of place reserved for encounter between human beings and the divine.

American churches and synagogues between the mid-nineteenth and mid-twentieth centuries more often than not appropriated styles of European inspiration ranging from Gothic splendor to Baroque exuberance to Georgian and classical styles to Victorian Romanticism including a revival of Moorish design for synagogues in the post–Civil War era. Designs tended toward eclecticism and nostalgia. The visual focal point in Protestant churches includes the pulpit and altar; in Roman Catholic churches the altar and tabernacle for the reserved Eucharist, which, prior to the Second Vatican Council in the early 1960s, functioned as a single elaborate unit; and in synagogues the ark containing the Torah scrolls and the bîmah, or reader's platform from which the scrolls are read.

Almost without exception the interiors in Meek's photographs reveal a symmetry of arrangement, with equilateral balance of all elements, even down to the identical flower arrangements flanking the central altar or ark. It is almost as if symmetry, balance, and equilibrium assert a surety, a stability, a steadfastness, a conviction that cannot be swayed or moved. The place is a still point in a chaotic world.

x

Images of Christ or the saints, or angels, or of narrative events from scripture, satisfy complex human needs. Their role has not been without controversy in the history of Christianity. Debates over their usefulness were generally settled by the early Middle Ages, at which time it was determined that images serve as occasions for encounter with the holy. Images are not venerated because of the richness of their materials or the splendor of their craftsmanship. They serve to point to a reality beyond and much larger than the image itself. An image of Mary is a pointer to the person of Mary, to something about who she is. A tangible image reminds the viewer that Mary was a mother who experienced all the anxieties of young parents about the safety of their children, and who ultimately watched her son suffer and die. She was no stranger to suffering and grief, and thus can be a comfort to others who endure difficult times. An image of Christ as the Good Shepherd is never about a portrait of Jesus, but rather an opportunity to contemplate the One who shepherds his sheep, his people, and to find one's place within that flock. A representation, no matter the medium, directs one's attention in a particular here and now to the larger idea or presence. In a mysterious way, images allow one to enter into the procession of all who have gone before in faith, and to dialogue with those whose images one encounters. They serve as memory joggers to larger stories, and in places of worship allow one time and place to connect with the truths and insights of their stories. Meek's photographs of such images evoke the mystery and often solitude of such moments. The photographs serve as a subsequent layer to jog memories of past encounters and experiences with these icons, wall paintings, or statues.

Regardless of the apparent subject of Meek's photographs, light provides the lens through which all images are captured. Elusive, fugitive, revelatory, immaterial, intangible, light nevertheless bears the weight of mystery. The serendipity of natural light's splashing across the floor shaping a cross happens by the intersection of the movement of the earth in relationship to the sun within a particular season at a specific time of day. A few minutes on either side of the moment, the image does not exist. But to see it etches an indelible memory of that place and time, a remarkable, yet fugitive moment of epiphany.

From antiquity holy men and women have perceived light as the presence of the divine. Familiar stories from the Hebrew Bible and the New Testament dramatically undergird the perception of light as the presence of God. In the narrative of Moses and the burning bush (Exodus 3:1–15), the voice of God emerges from the flames, directing Moses to remove his sandals, for he stands on holy ground. From within the light God discloses to Moses the intimacy of his holy name. At the baptism of Christ in the Jordan River the heavens open, the spirit of God descends as a dove, and the voice of God speaks to Jesus from the sky rent asunder, saying, "This is my beloved son in whom I am well pleased. Listen to Him." Once more revelation occurs washed in light. Flashes of light throw Saul to the ground, blinding him on his way to Damascus (Acts

9:1–17), a life-changing event ultimately transforming Saul the persecutor of the disciples of Christ into Paul the disciple of Christ.

Christ describes himself as the light of the world and source of life (John 1:12). The most ancient Christian hymn, *Phos Hilaron*, is sung in the evening at lamp lighting. Opening with the words "O radiant light, O sun divine. . . ," it is still sung in Eastern and Western Christian churches today at vespers.

In the French Gothic era of the twelfth century the art of stained glass blossomed into the direct service of religion. Abbot Suger justified the jewel-like windows at the rebuilt St. Denis royal monastery by describing how they marvelously transport the mind from the material to the immaterial world. As natural light passes through the colored glass it is transformed into something distinguishable, if not tangible. Such colored light suffuses the space with a palpable energy and divine presence. Several of Meek's photographs capture the elusive bits of color hovering in the air and softly settling on furniture and floors, as if the space and all that happens there are momentarily noticed and caressed by the divine. Light dramatically filters through cracks under doors and thrusts sharp-edged geometric patterns into interiors, while larger apertures under the right conditions allow clouds of light to hover as if anticipating the voice of God. Pools of light on the floor invite movement into that light, certainly a metaphor for transformation. Sometimes the light in the photographs settles on just an edge of an architectural detail, or the rim of an angel's wing, or the cover of a Bible, or the relief image on a tabernacle door, or a letter or two of an inscription. The viewer is silently but persuasively invited to focus for a moment on a detail. Light's power lies in the ambiguity of its content. Here the physics of light gives way to story and memory.

Some thirty-five hundred years ago Jacob declared the place of his dream the portal of heaven. This is yet one more place in the human story where divinity reveals itself amidst ordinary life. In Jacob's dream, God's messengers perpetually ascend and descend between earth and heaven's realm, confirming the inescapable truth that the dichotomy between sacred and profane is indeed a false premise. The marriage between heaven and earth is eternal and relentless. Meek's photographs unveil the often overlooked facets of the mystery of the holy and the human. His artist's eye explores the myriad details of the interiors of houses of worship, waiting for just the exact moment in which the serendipity of light dissolves any distinction between the ordinary and the holy. Viewers of Meek's photographs will be drawn to see things anew, or perhaps for the first time, to catch a glimpse of a long-forgotten moment's revelation that can touch the heart and renew a dialogue with the holy. As they remember encounters they have had in places such as these, Meek's photographs may inspire them, like Jacob, to proclaim that surely God is in this place.

Marchita B. Mauck

Altars, Chancels, and Sanctuaries

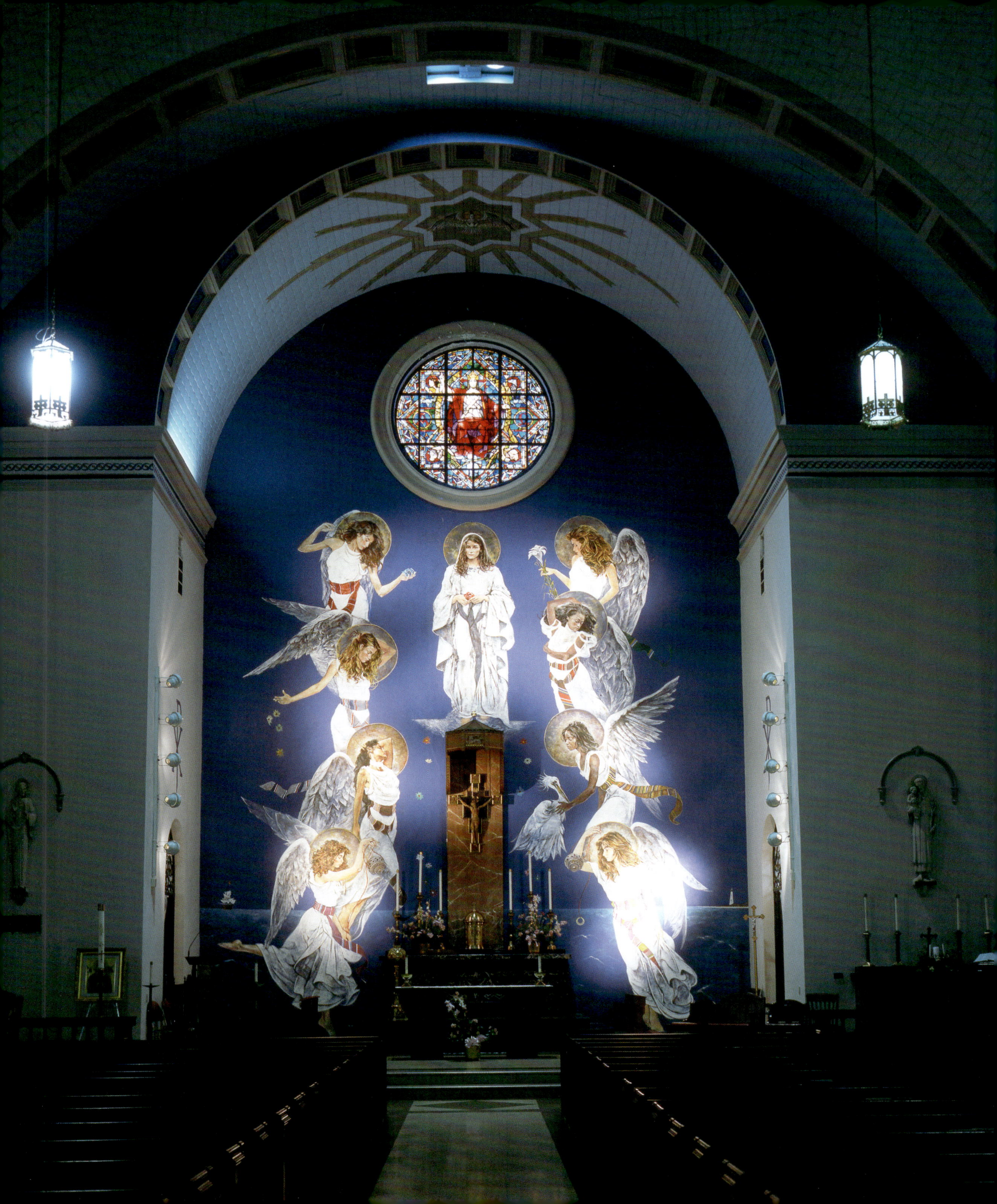

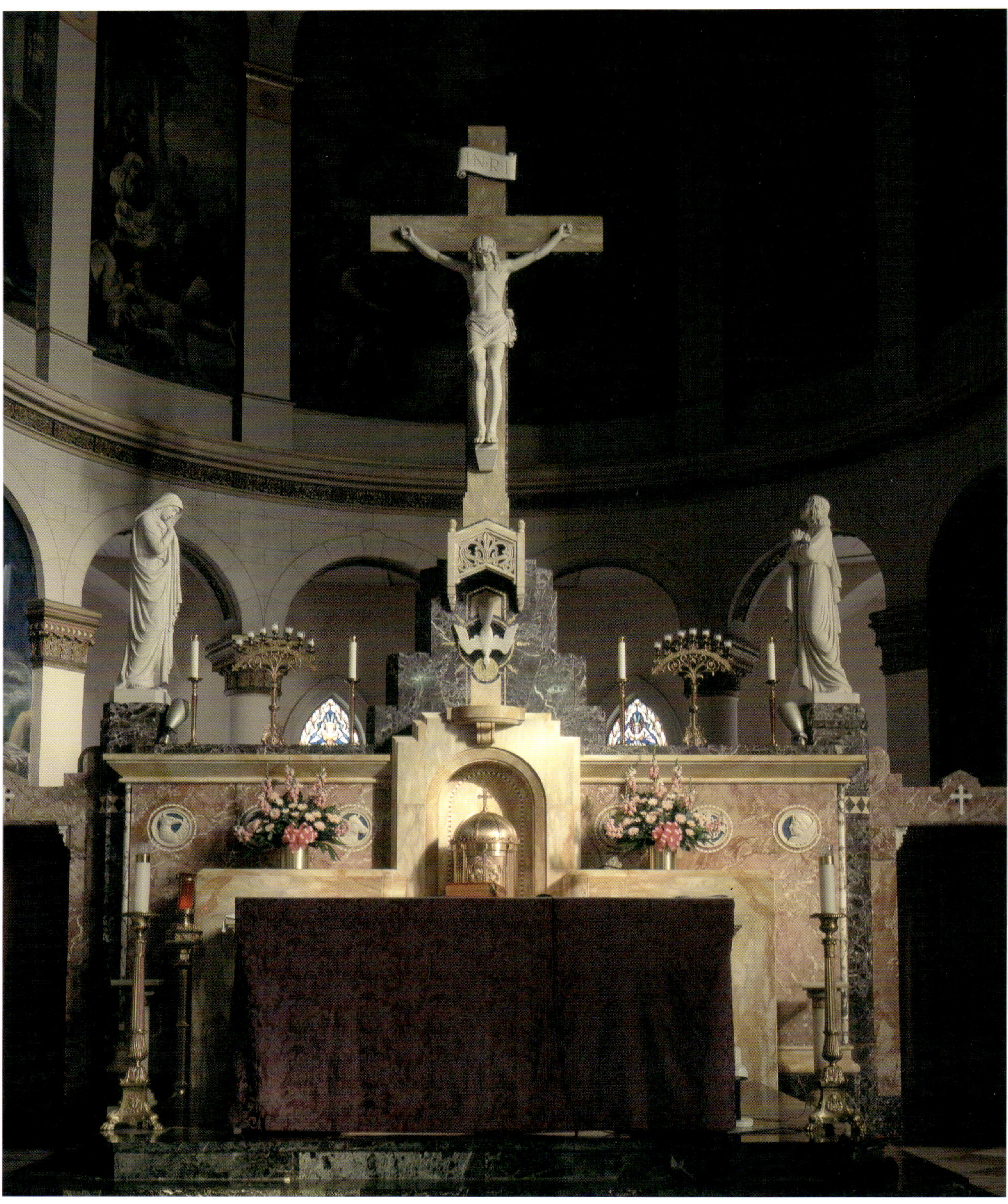

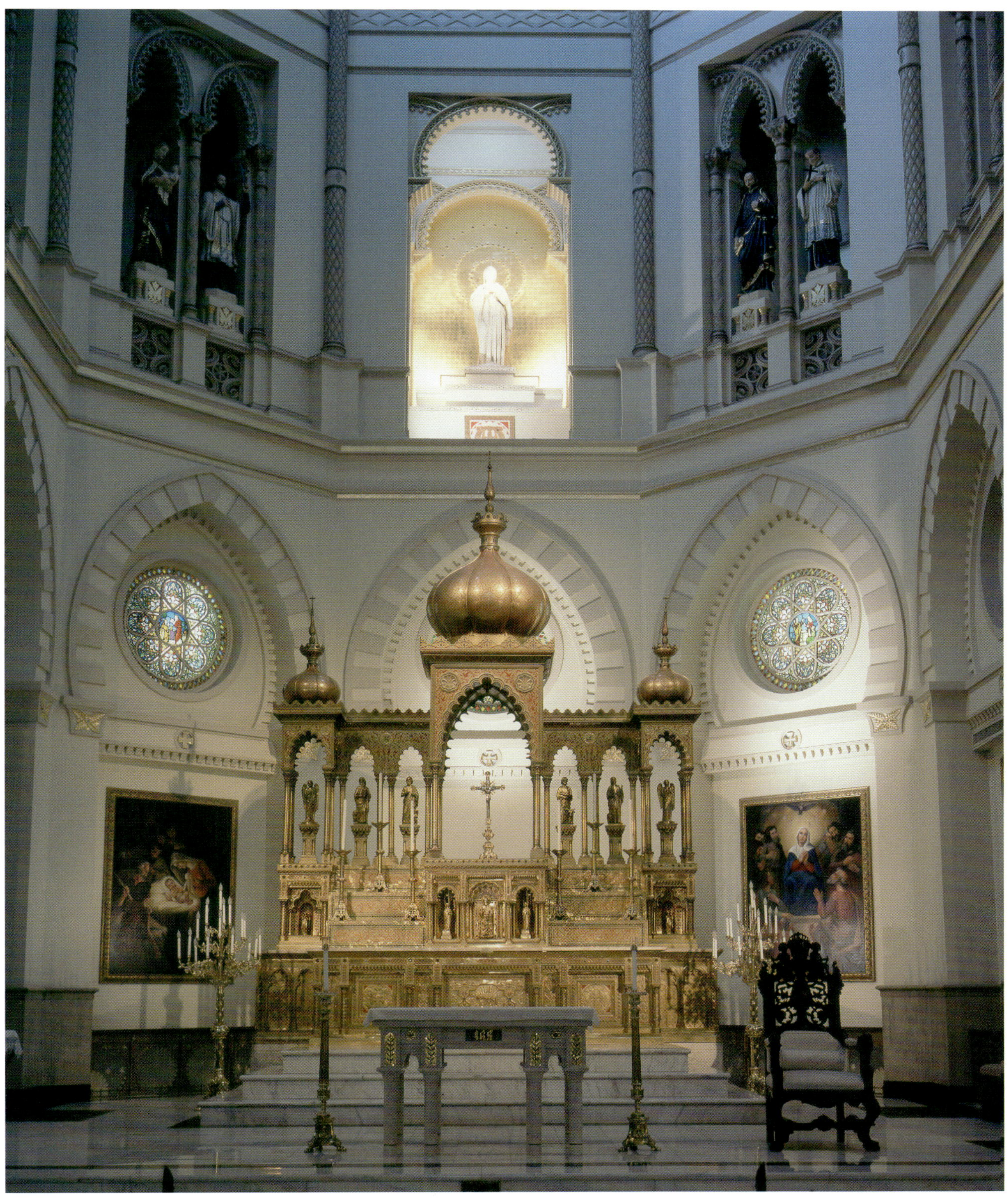

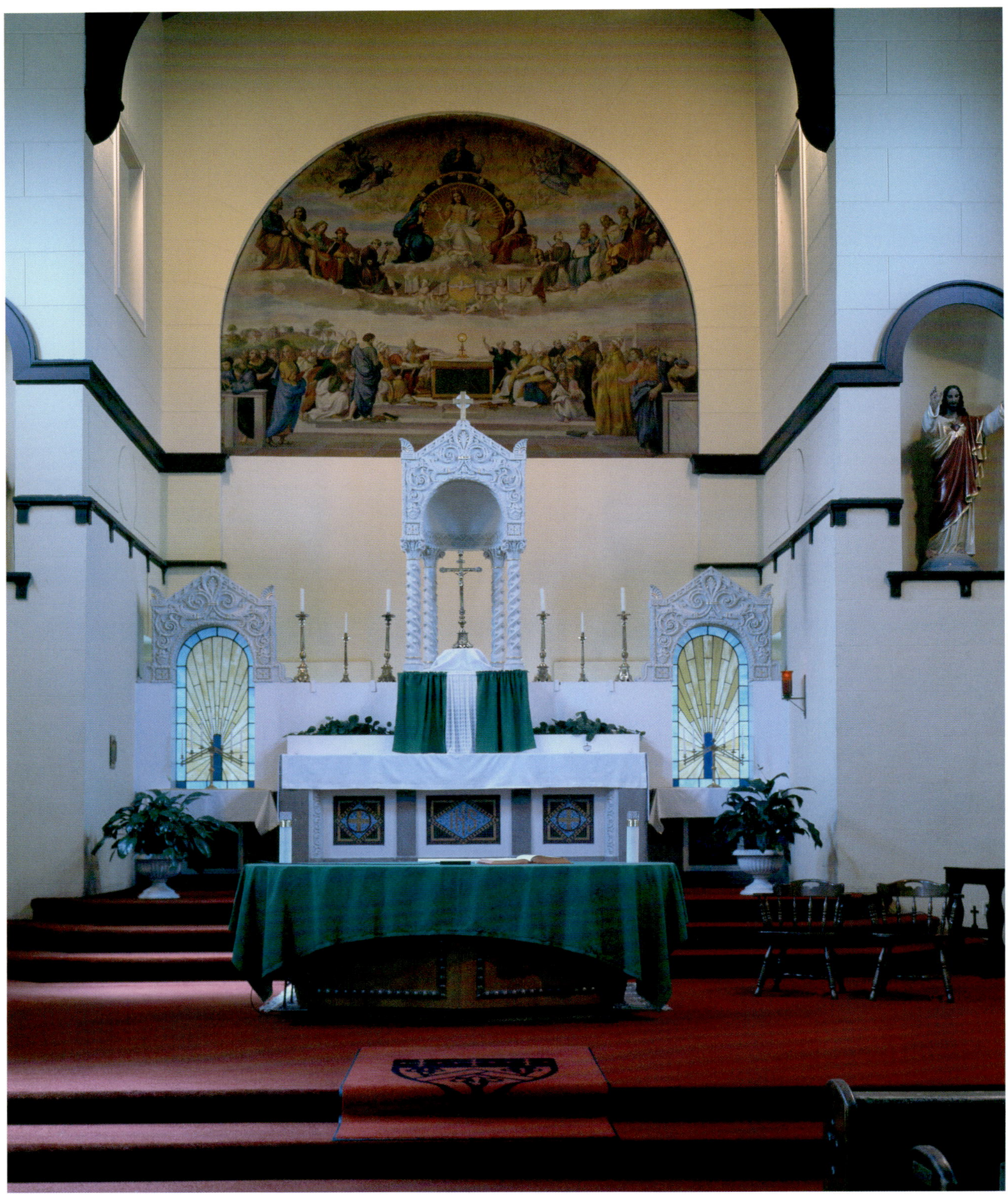

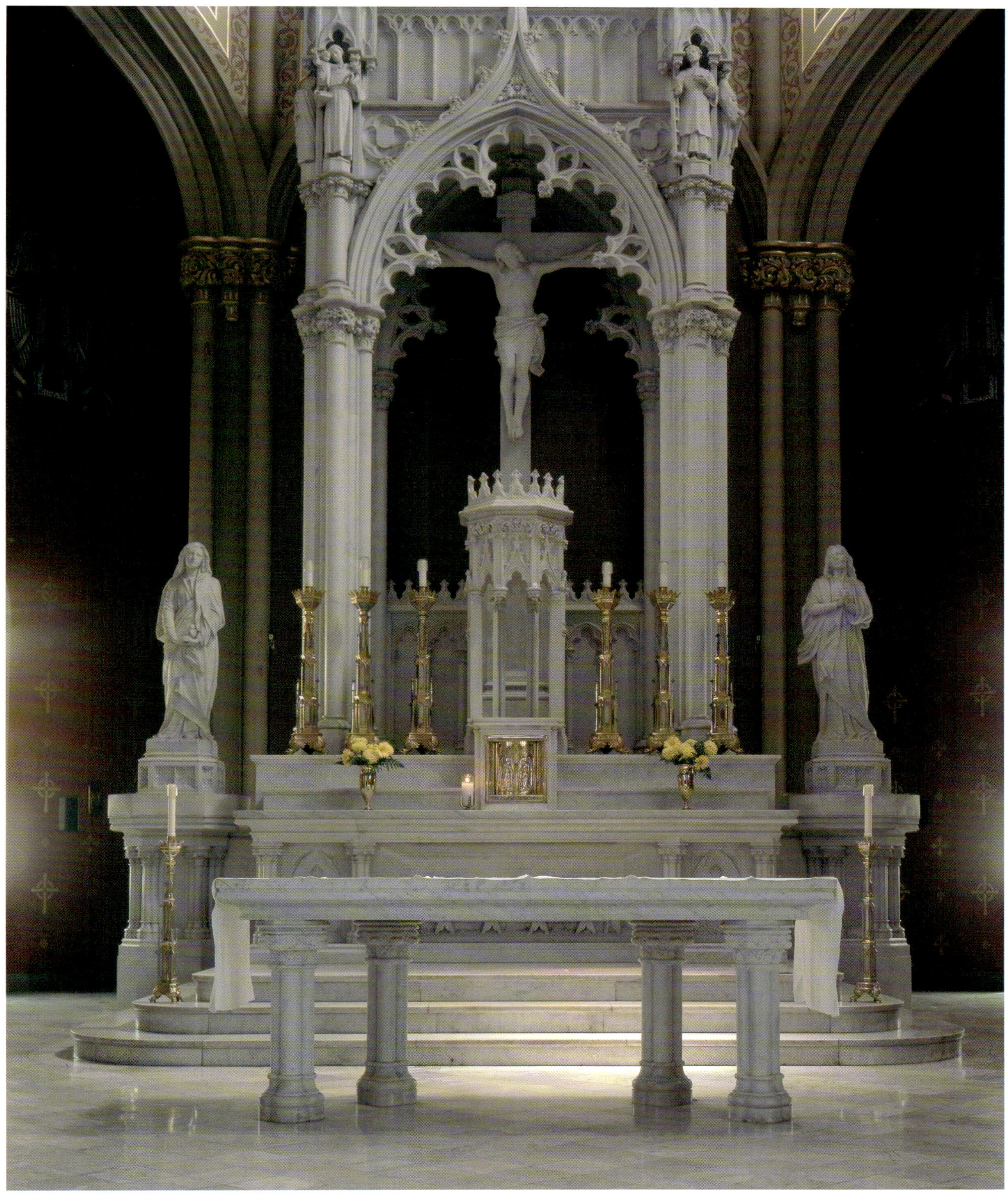

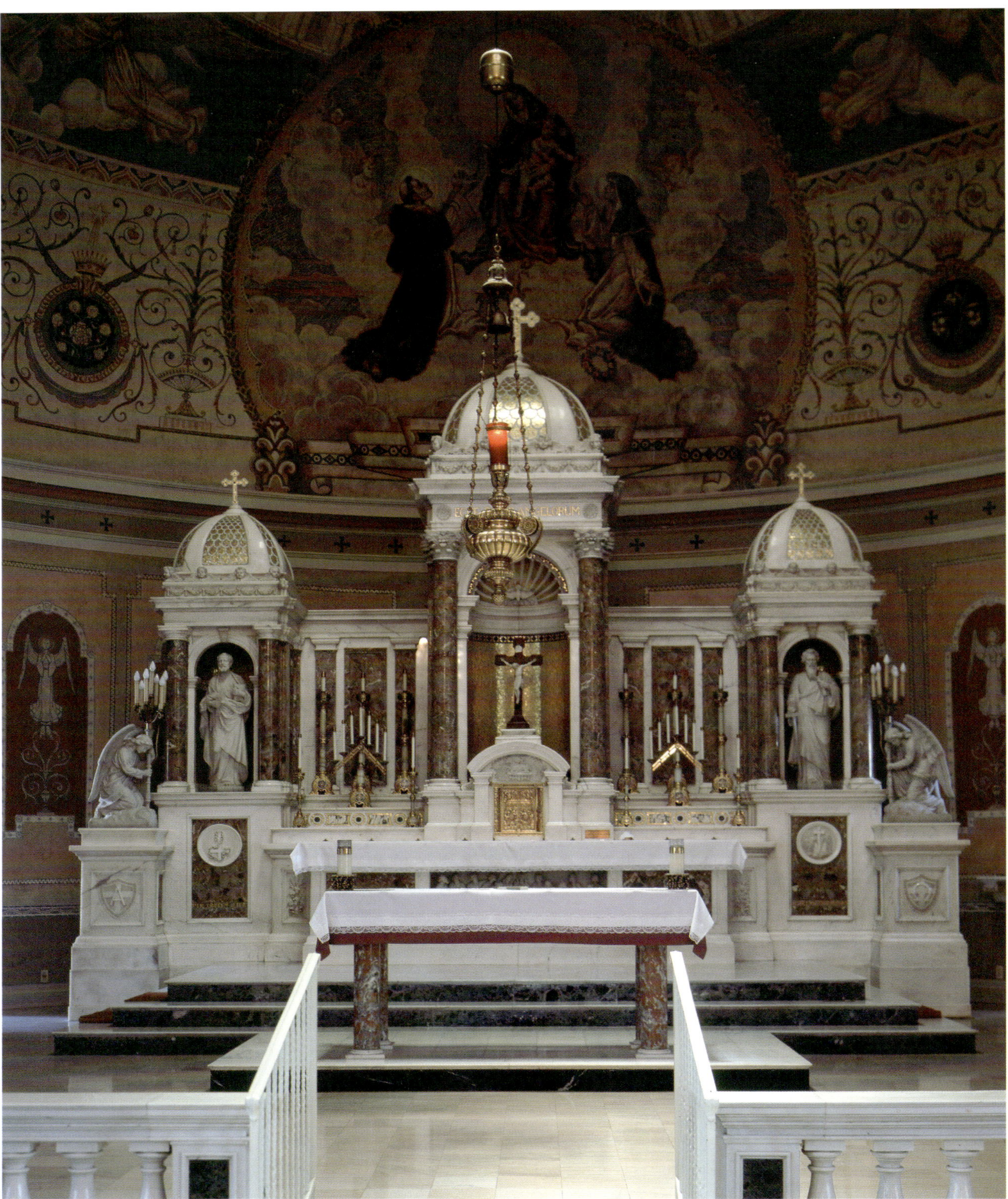

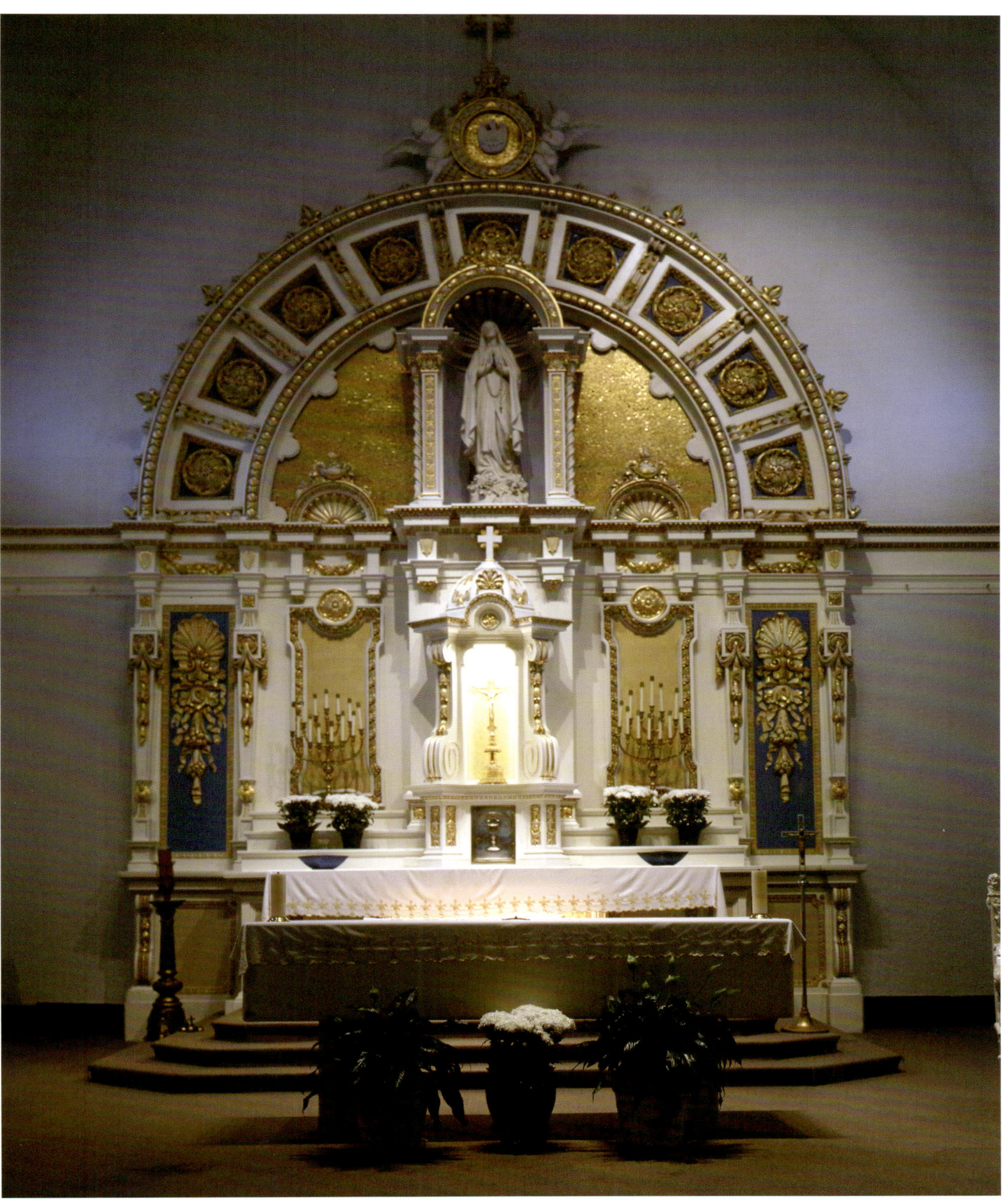

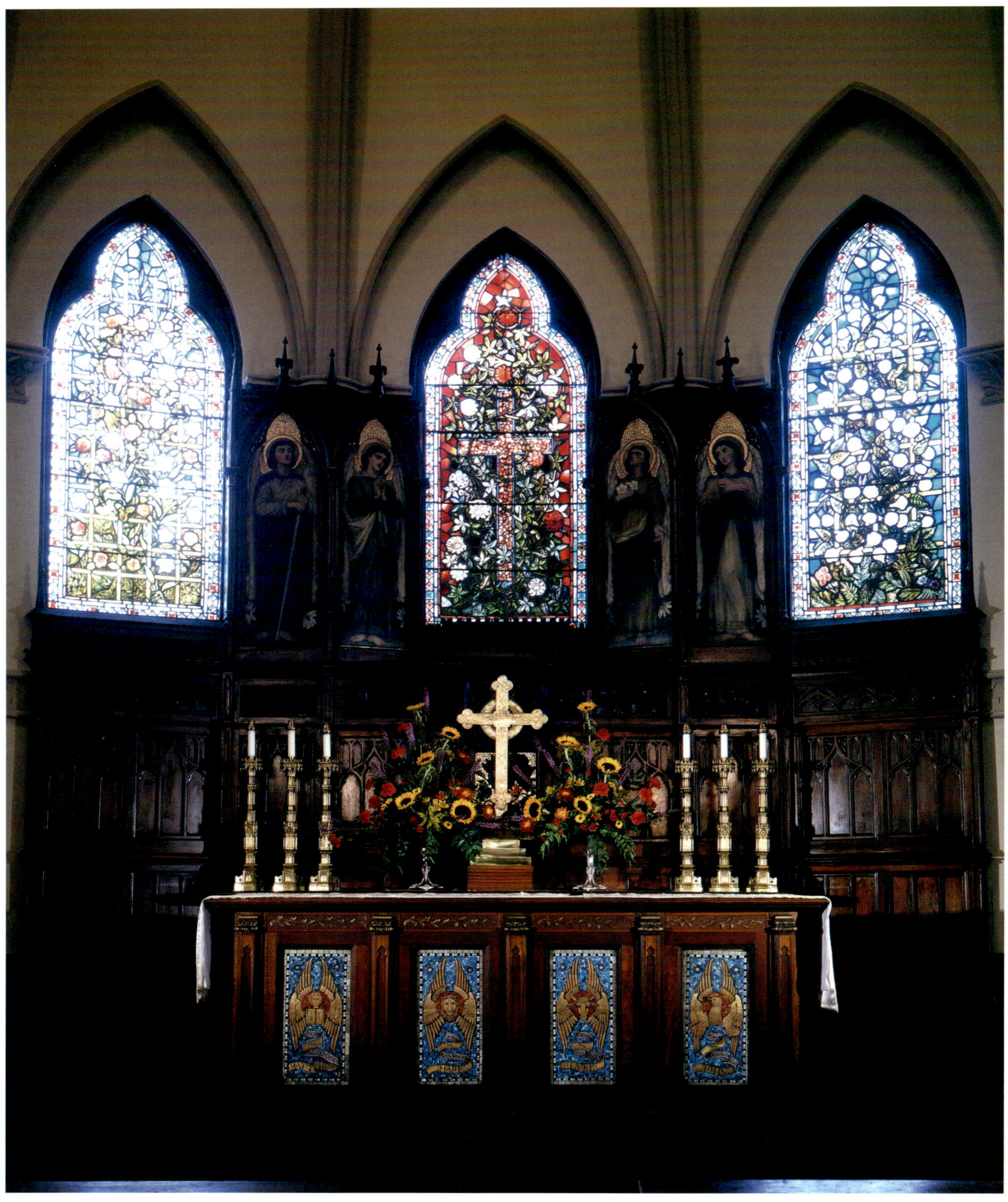

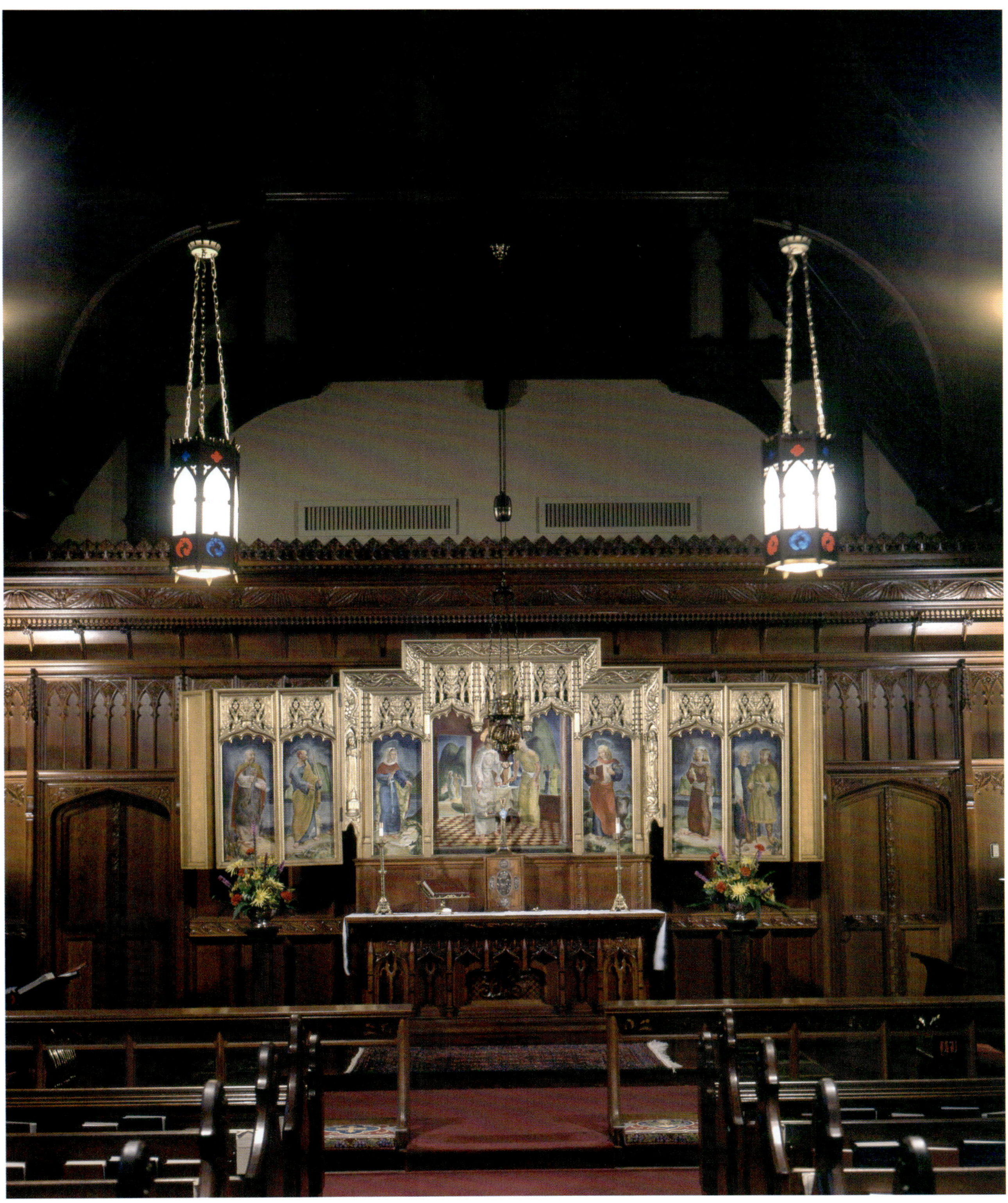

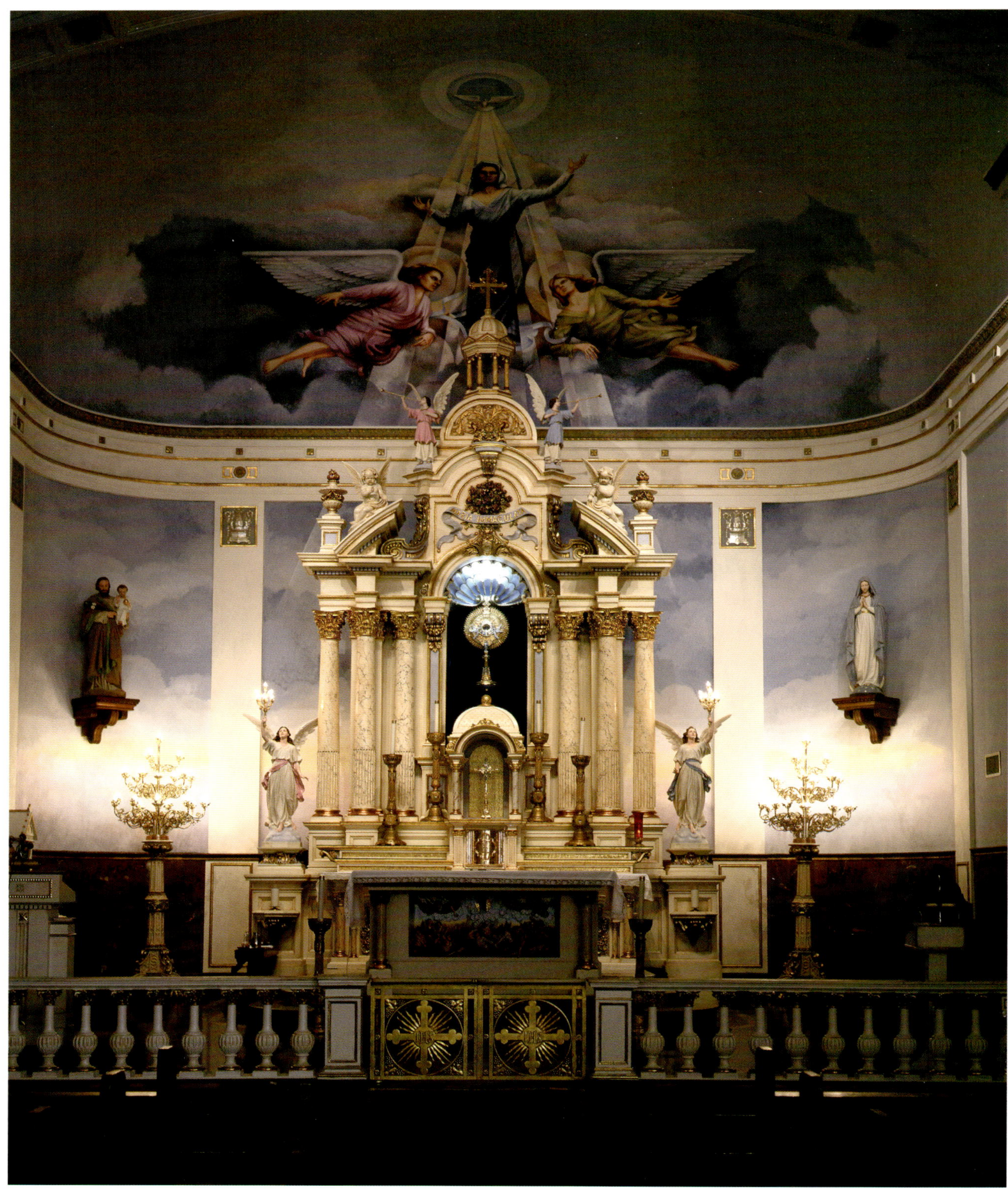

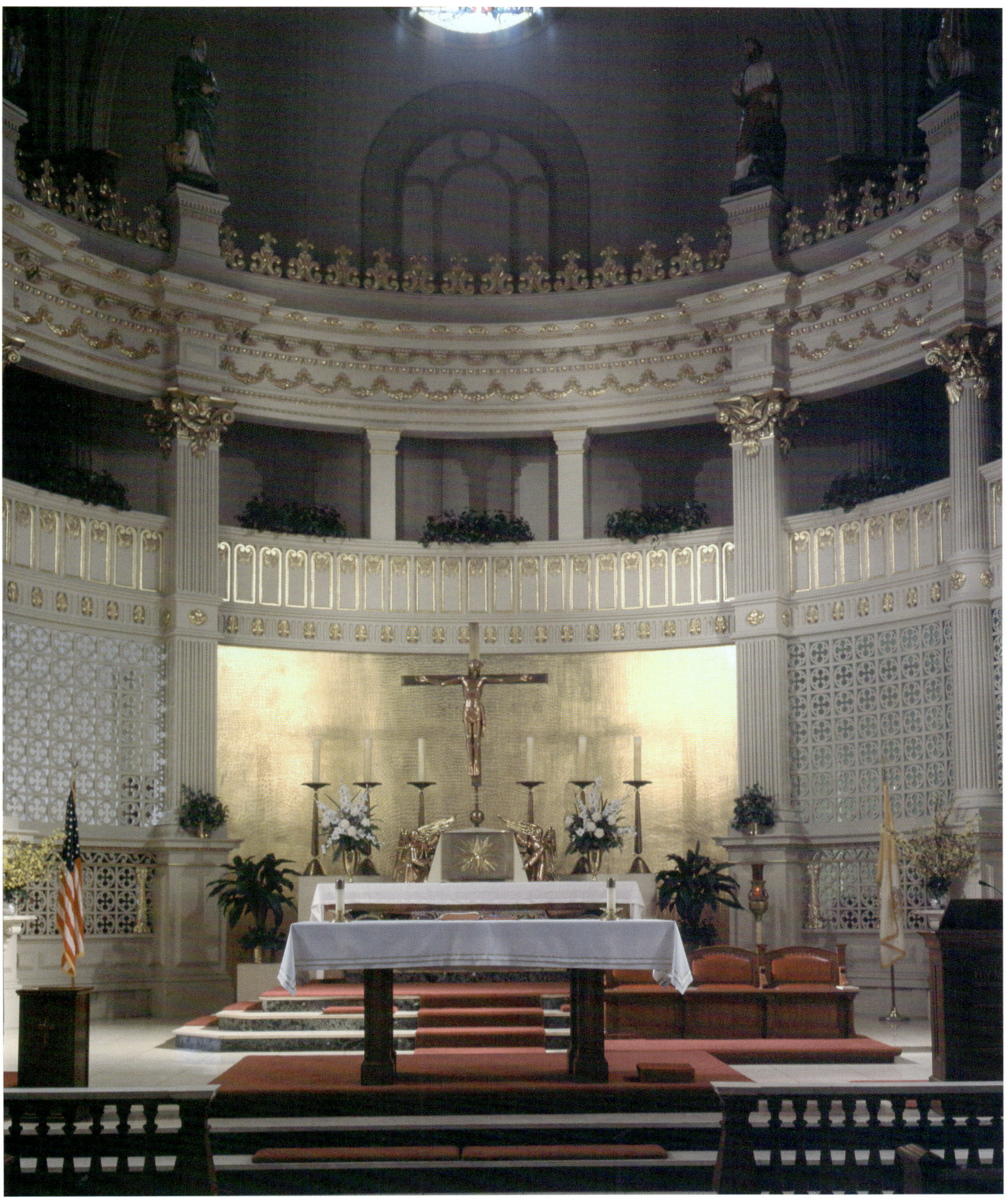

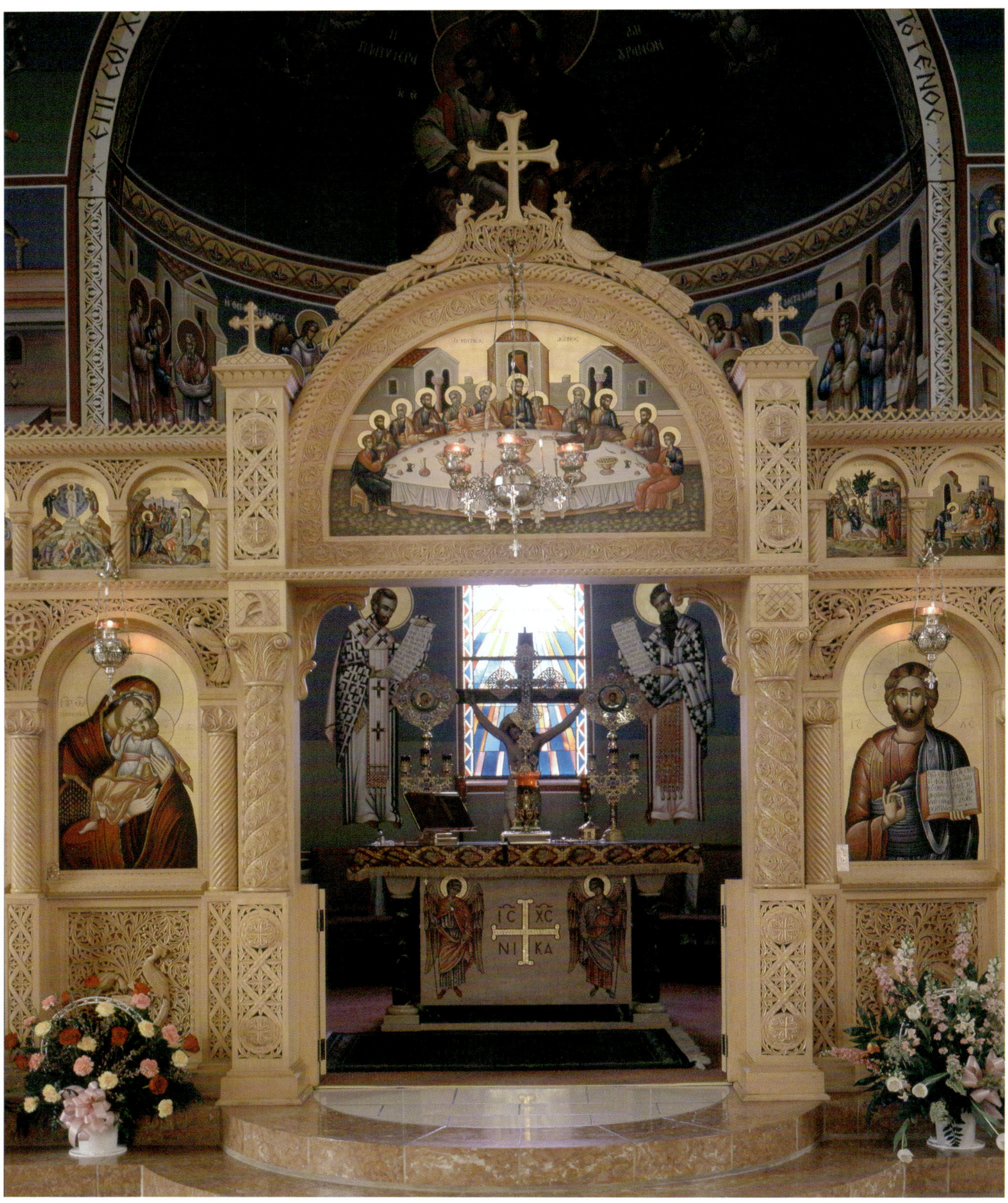

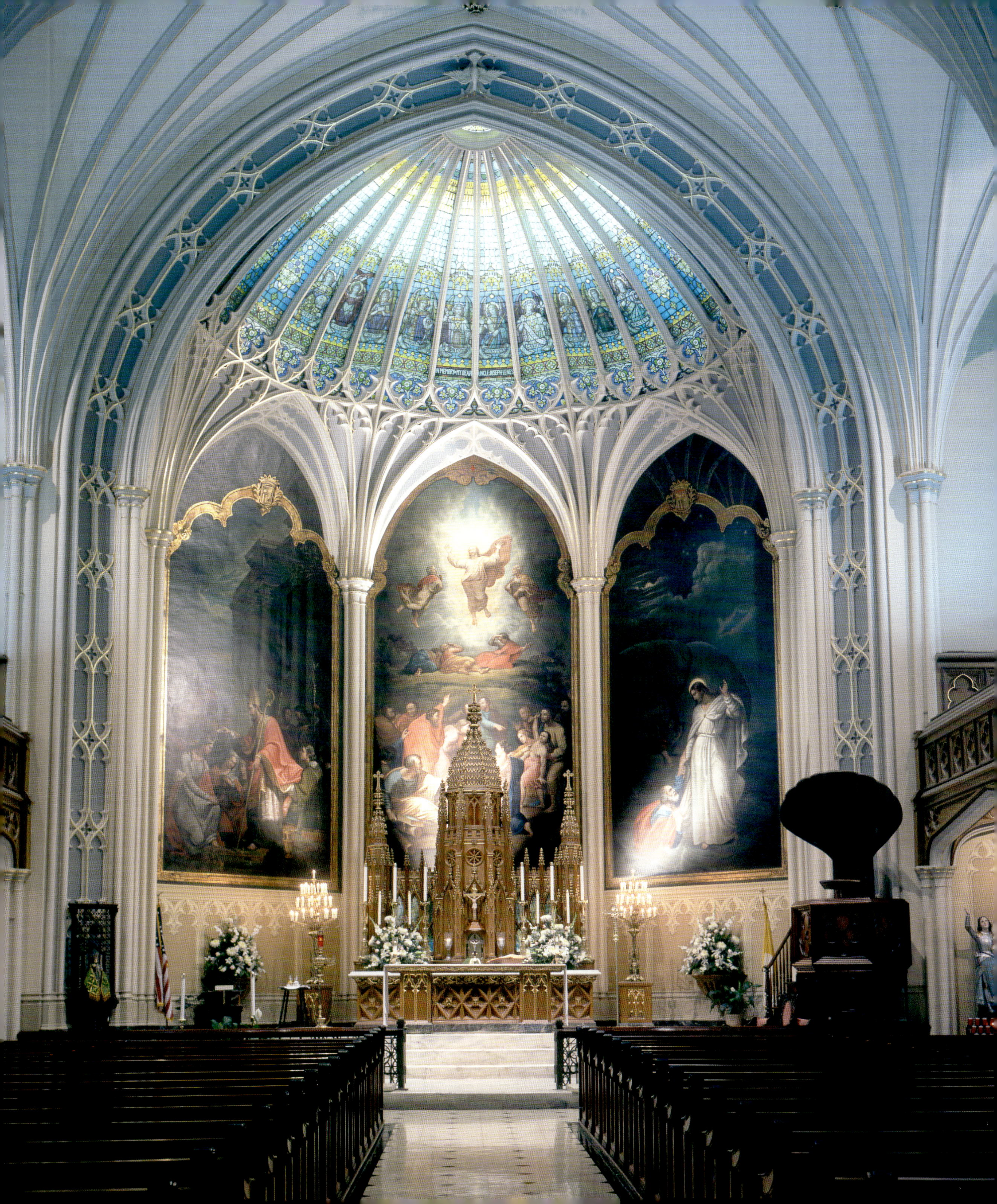

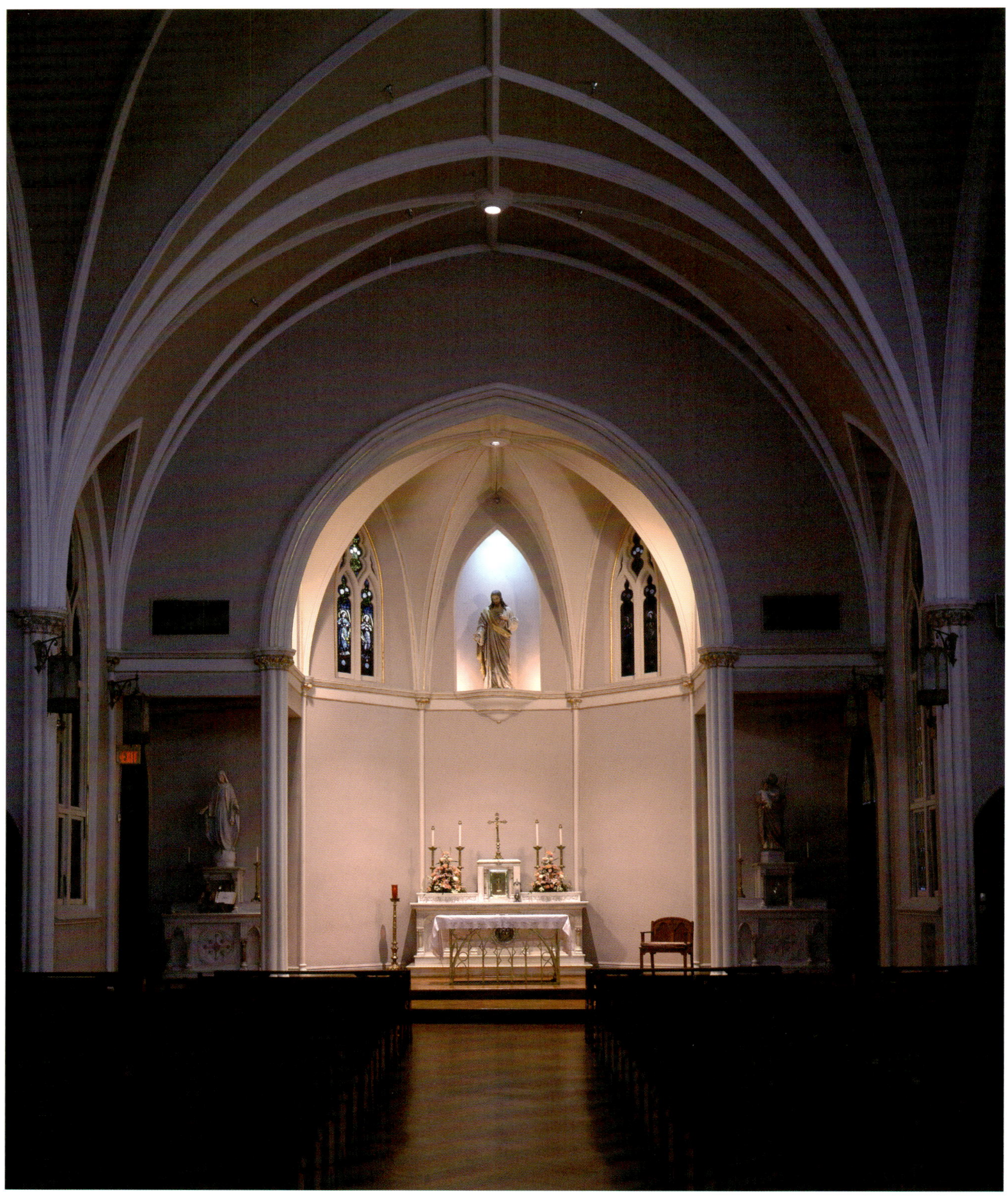

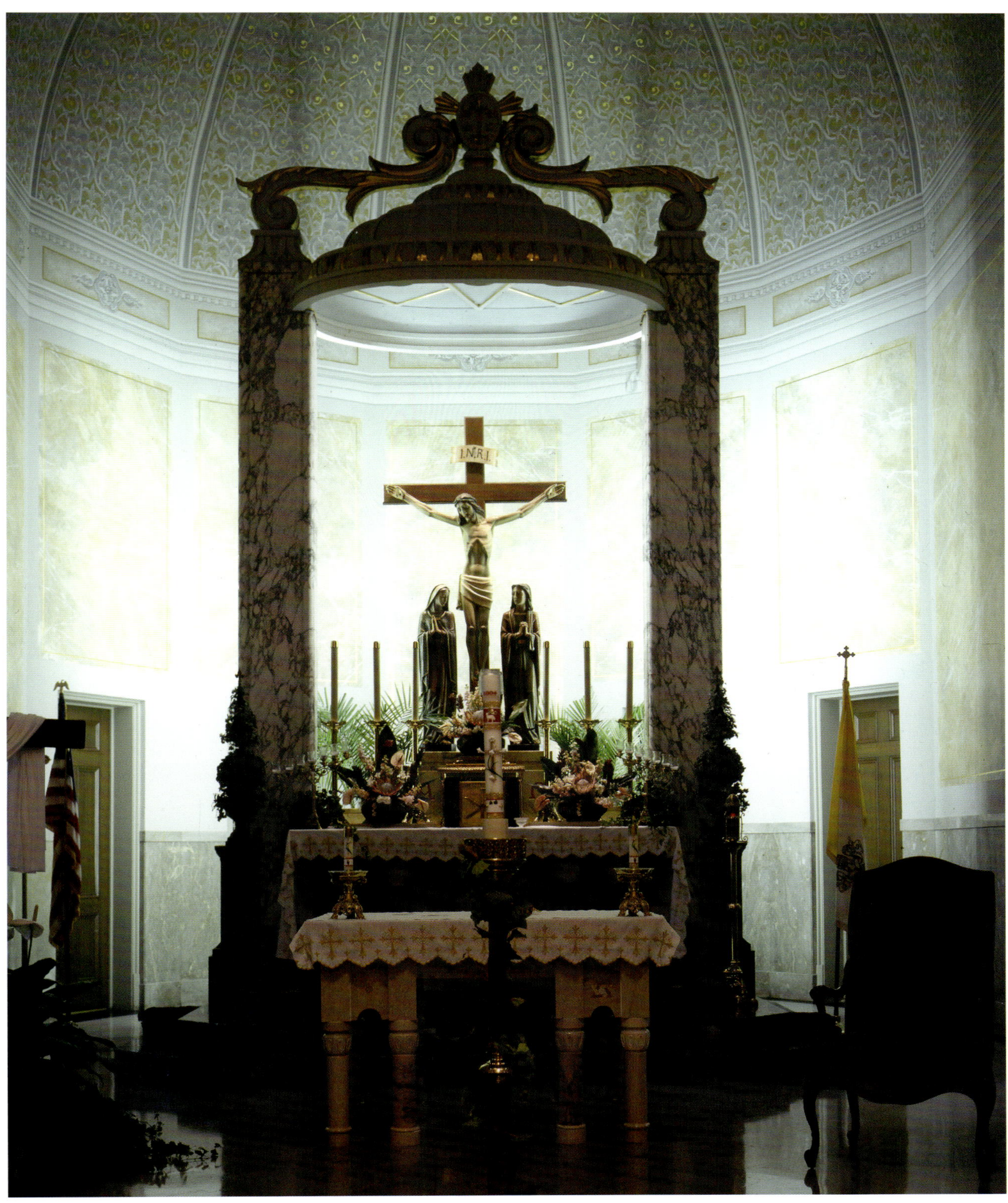

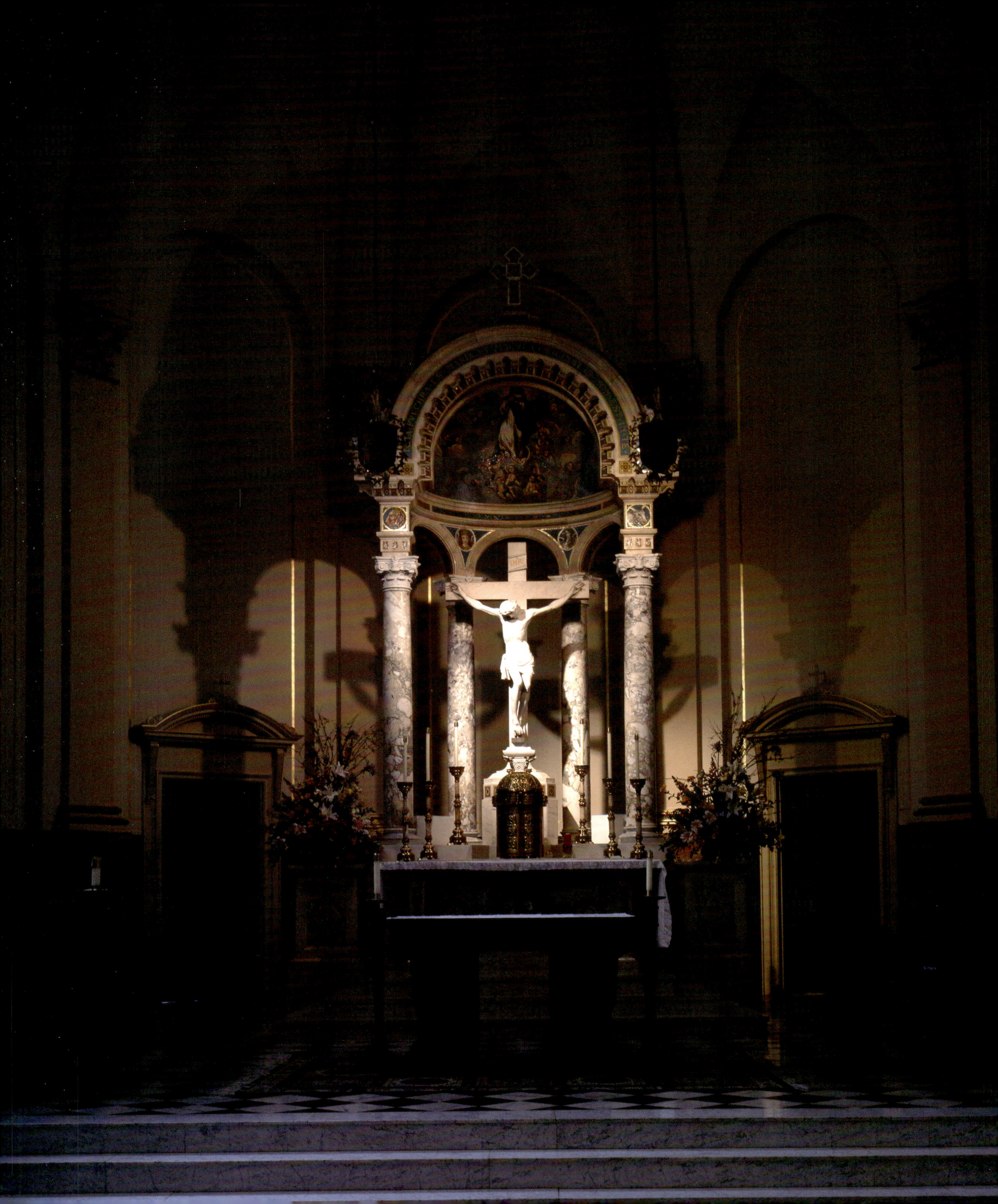

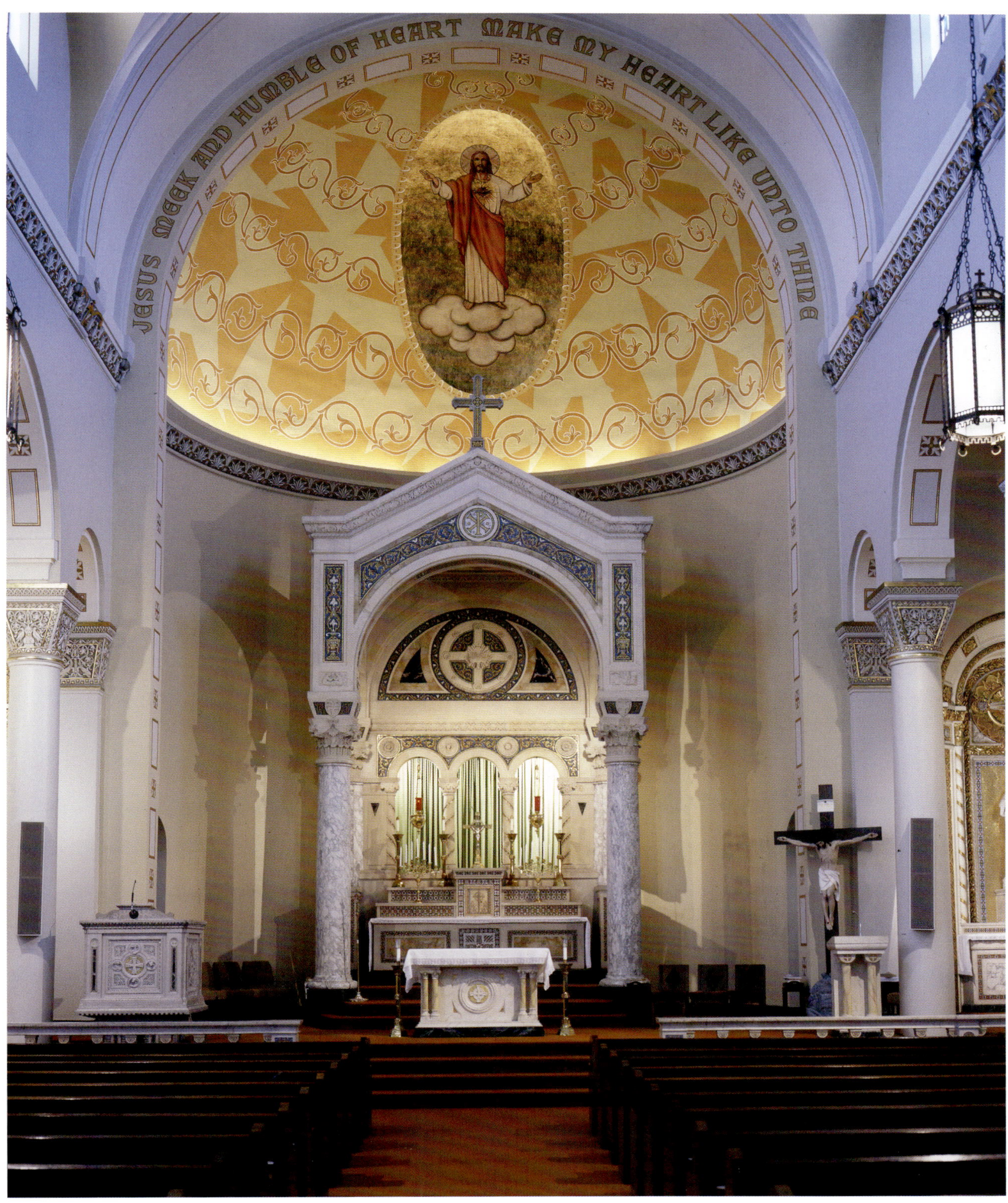

JESUS MEEK AND HUMBLE OF HEART MAKE MY HEART LIKE UNTO THINE

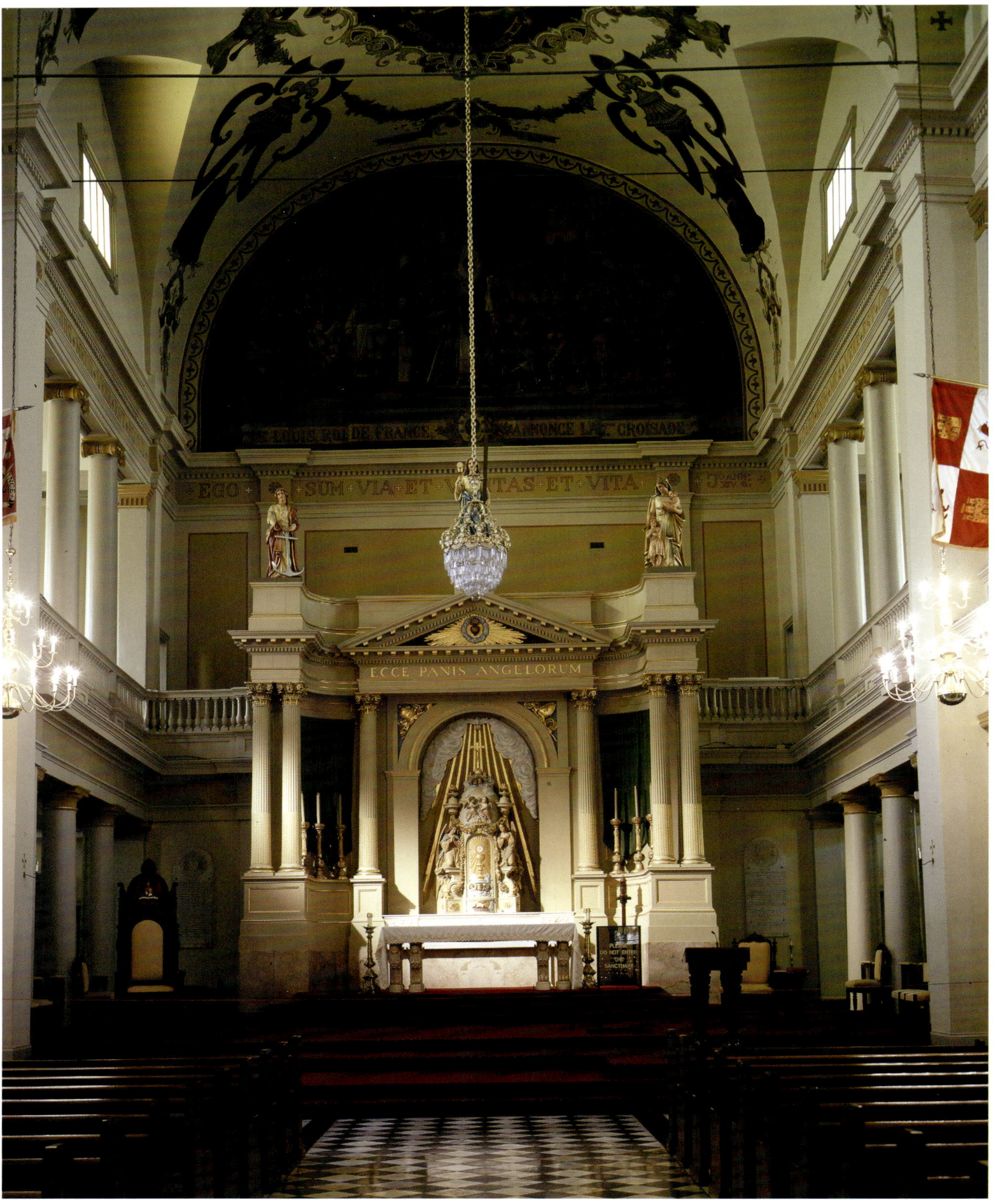

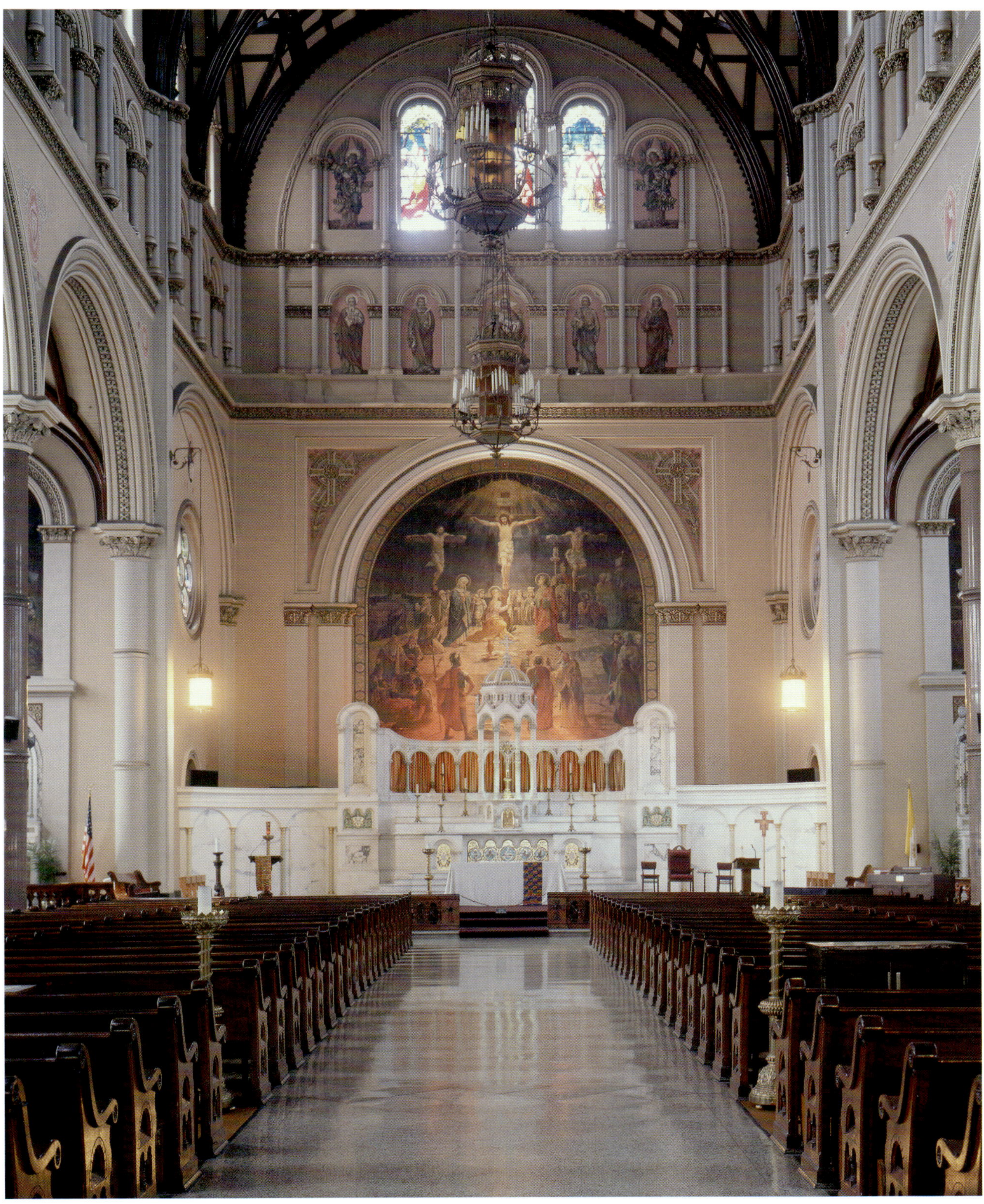

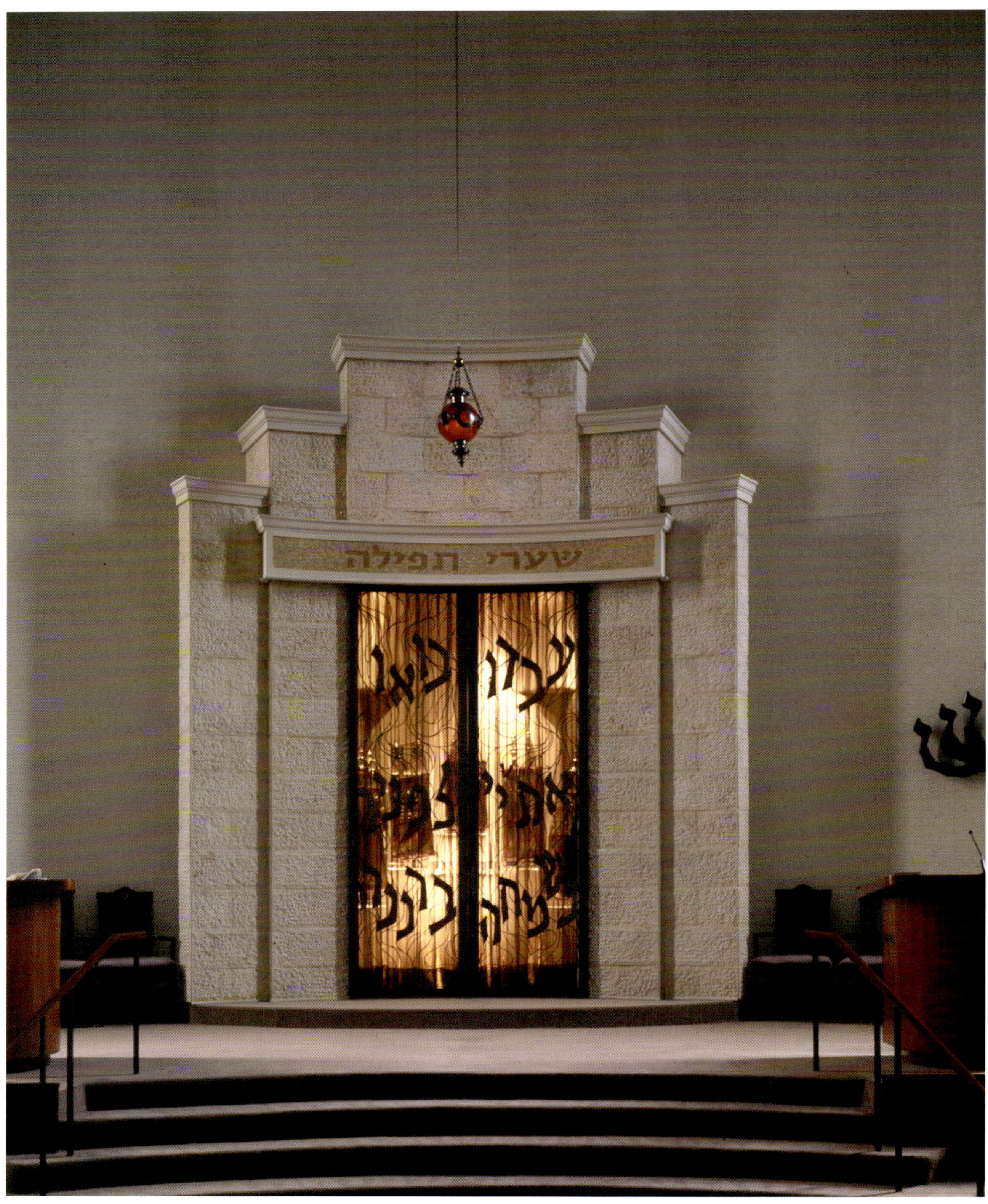

שערי תפילה

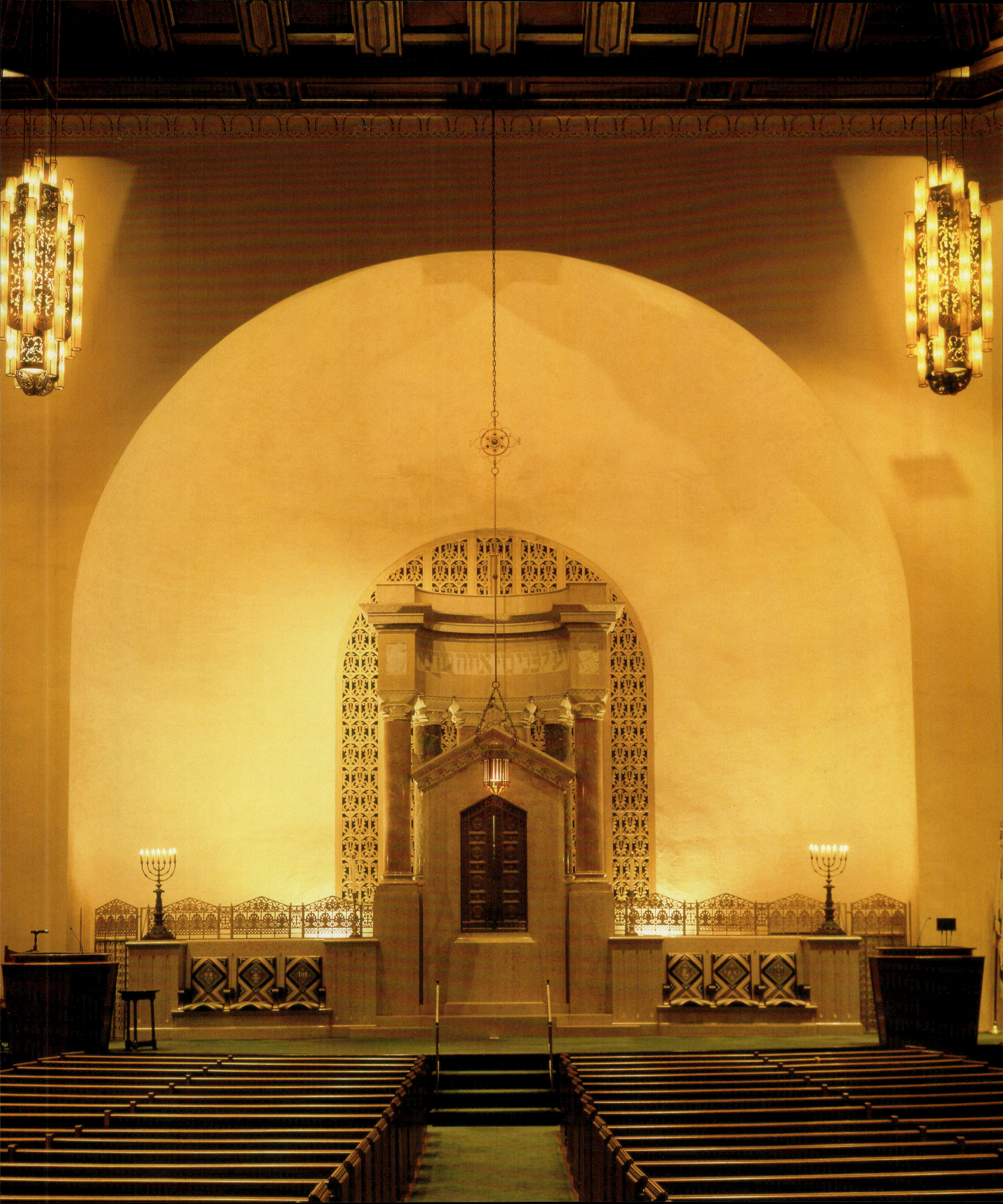

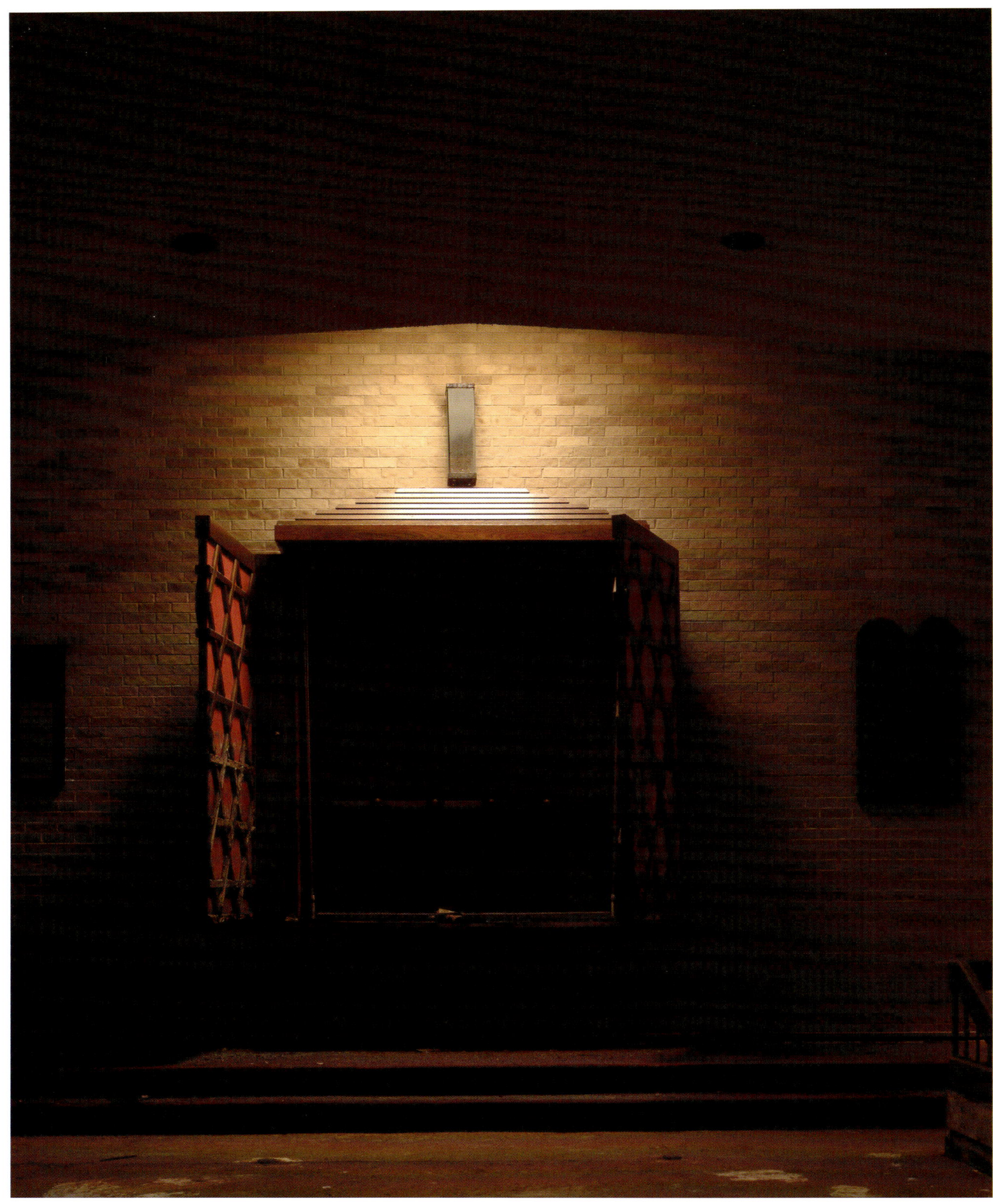

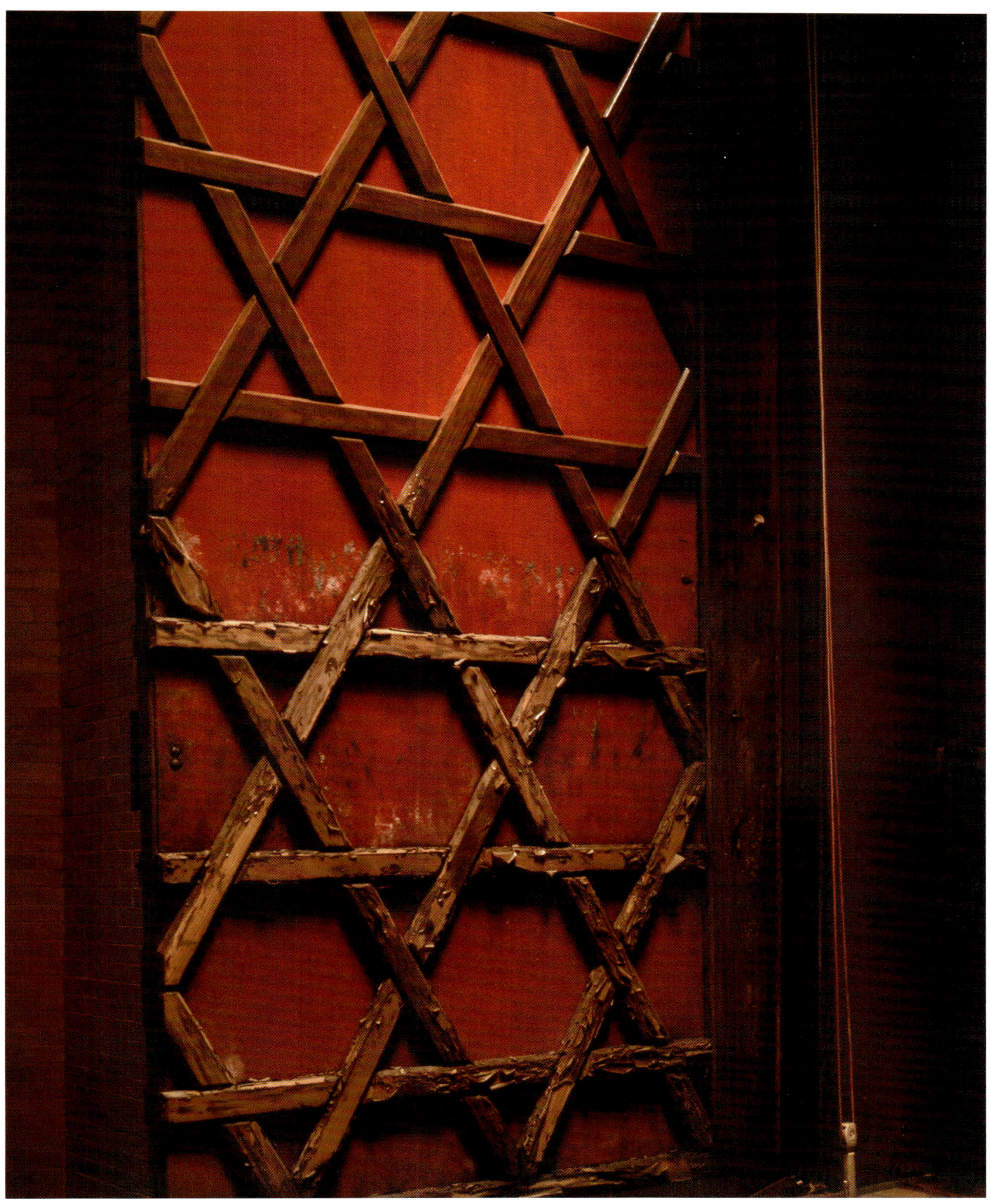

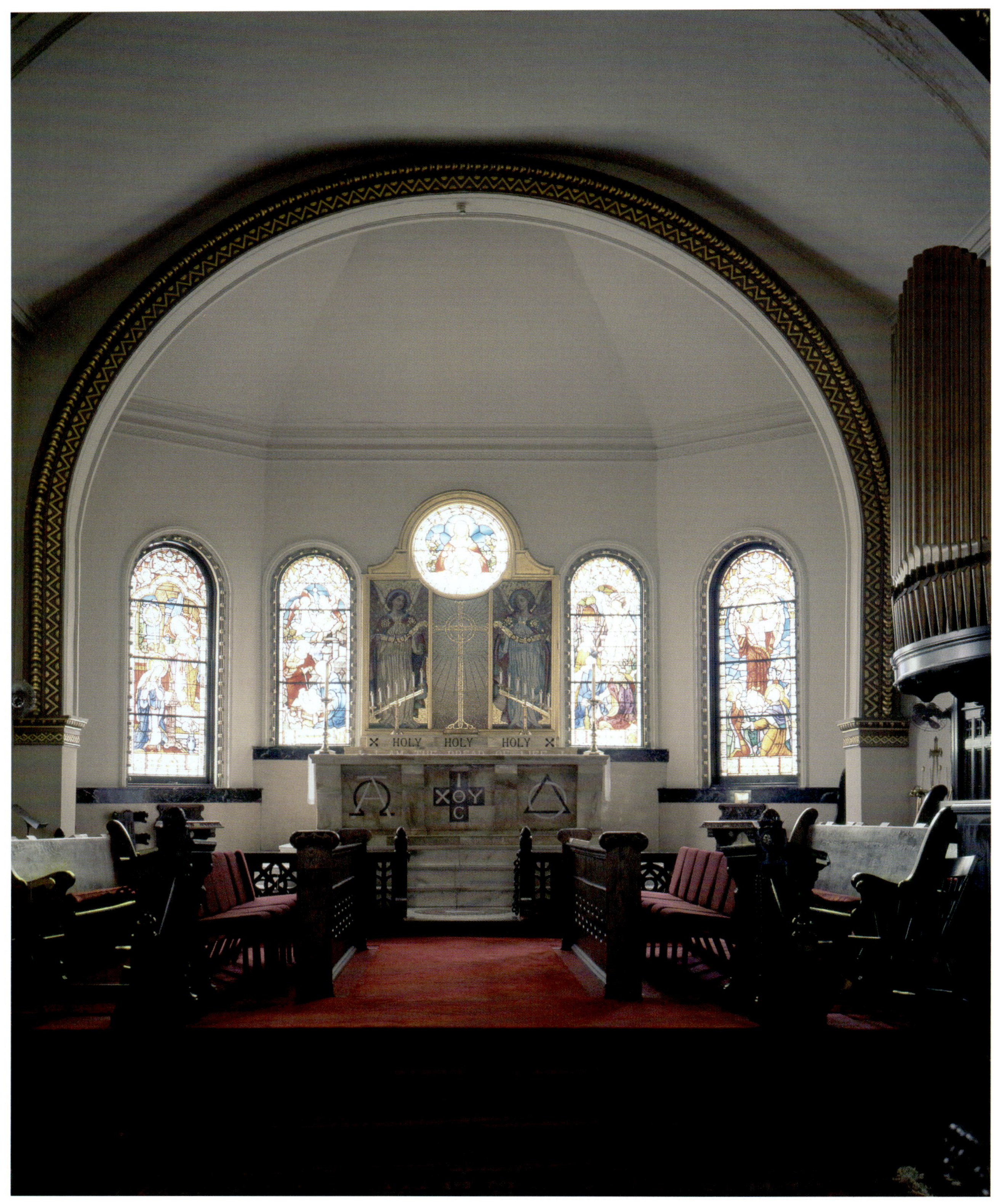

HOLY HOLY HOLY

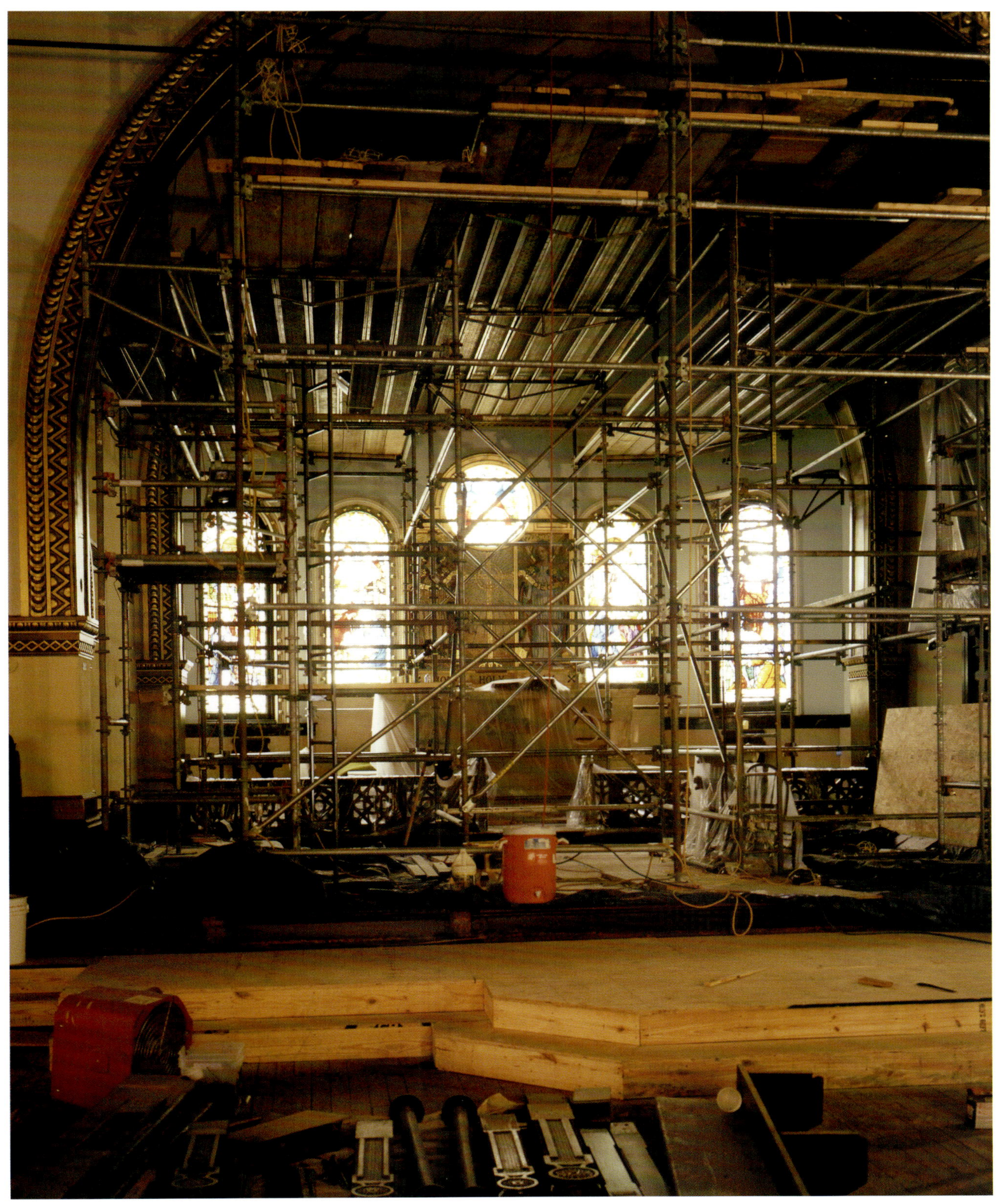

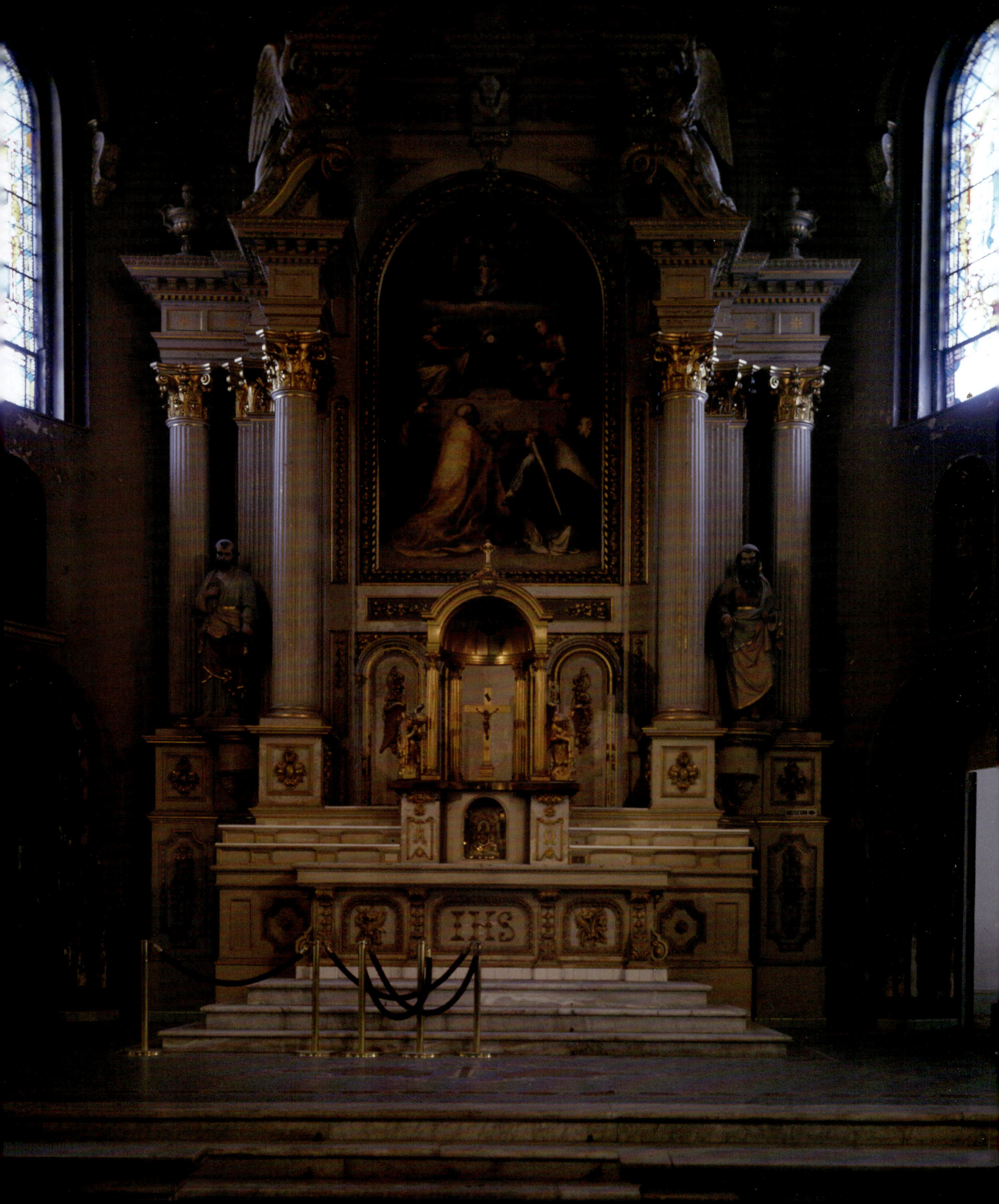

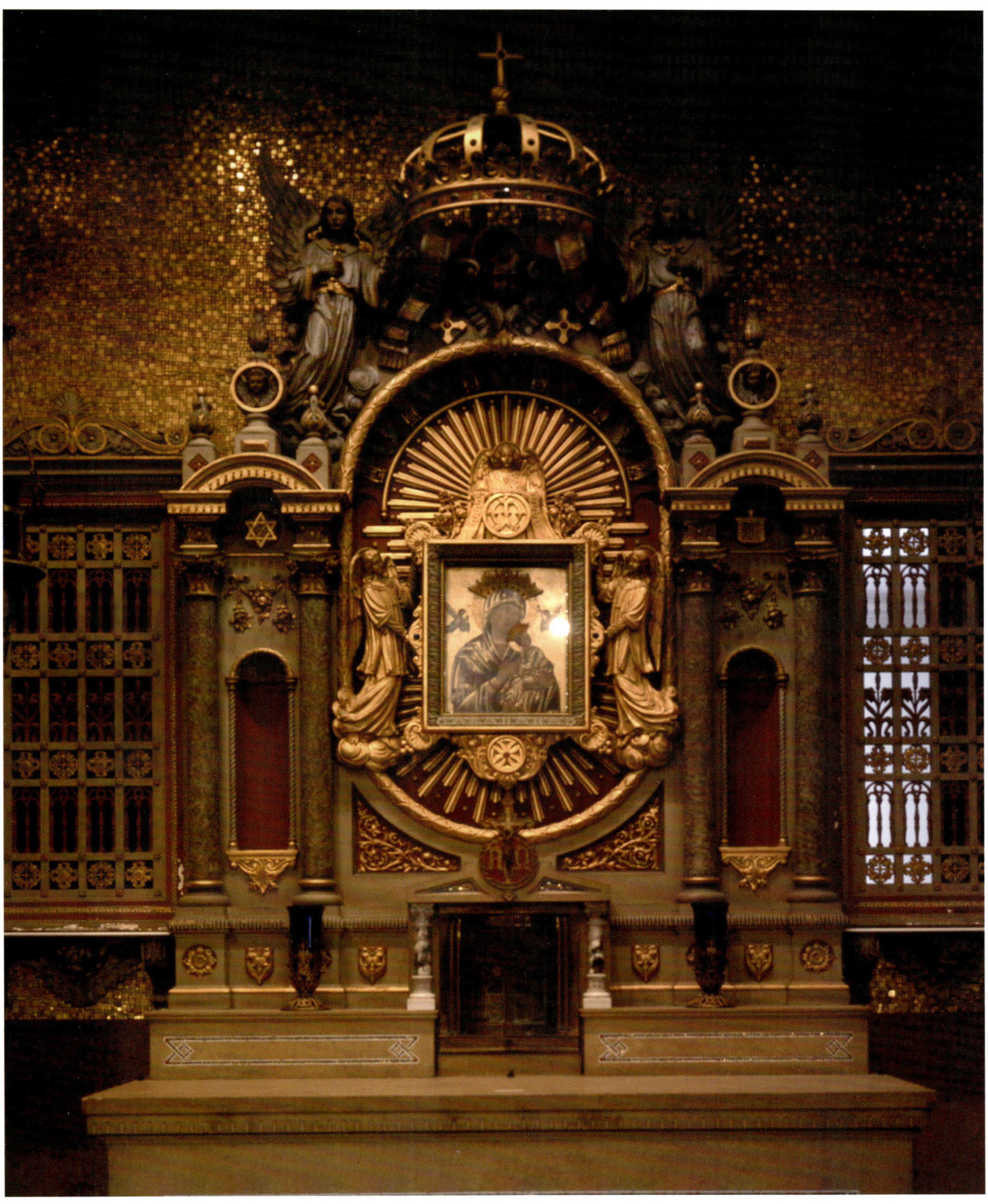

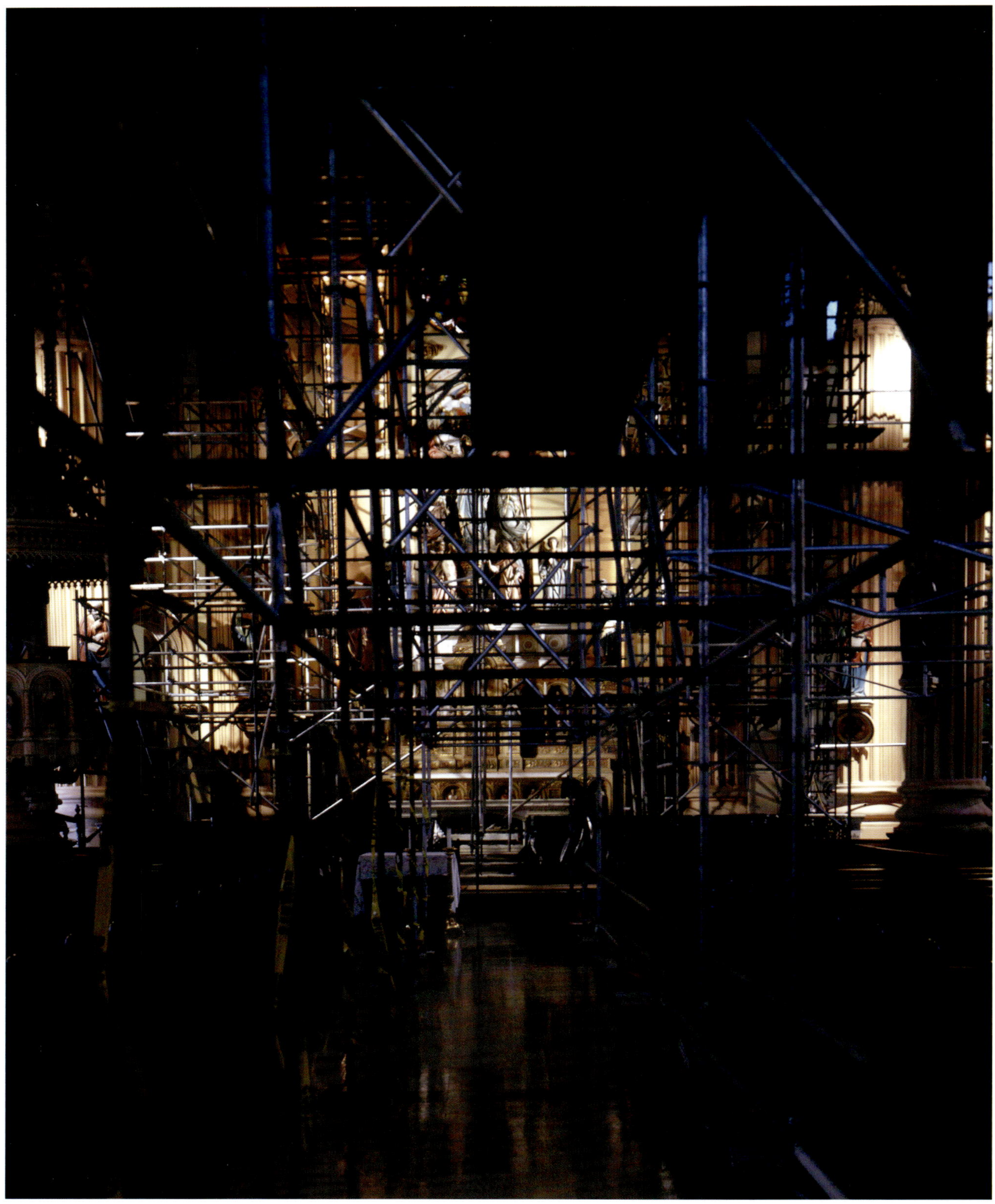

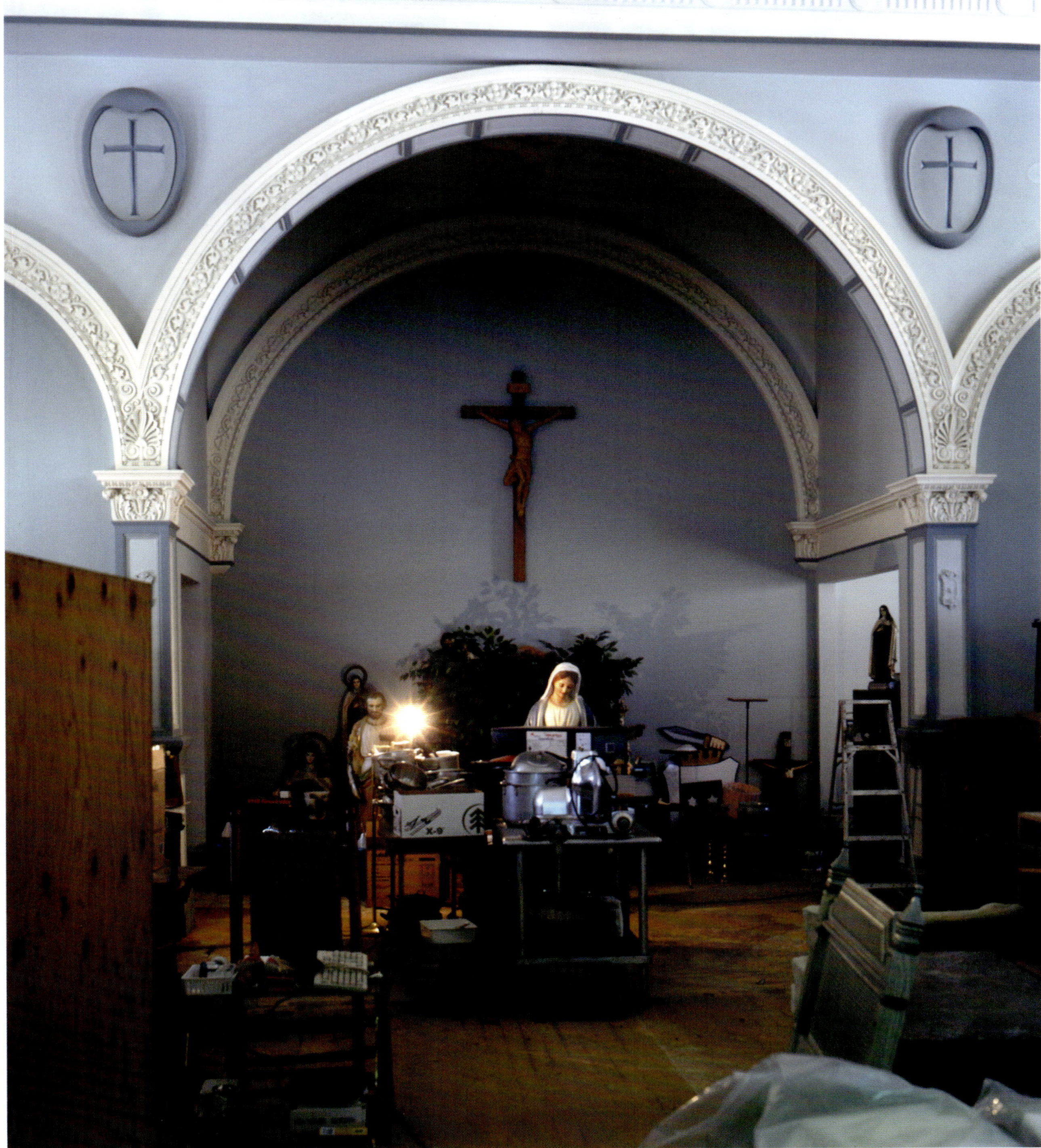

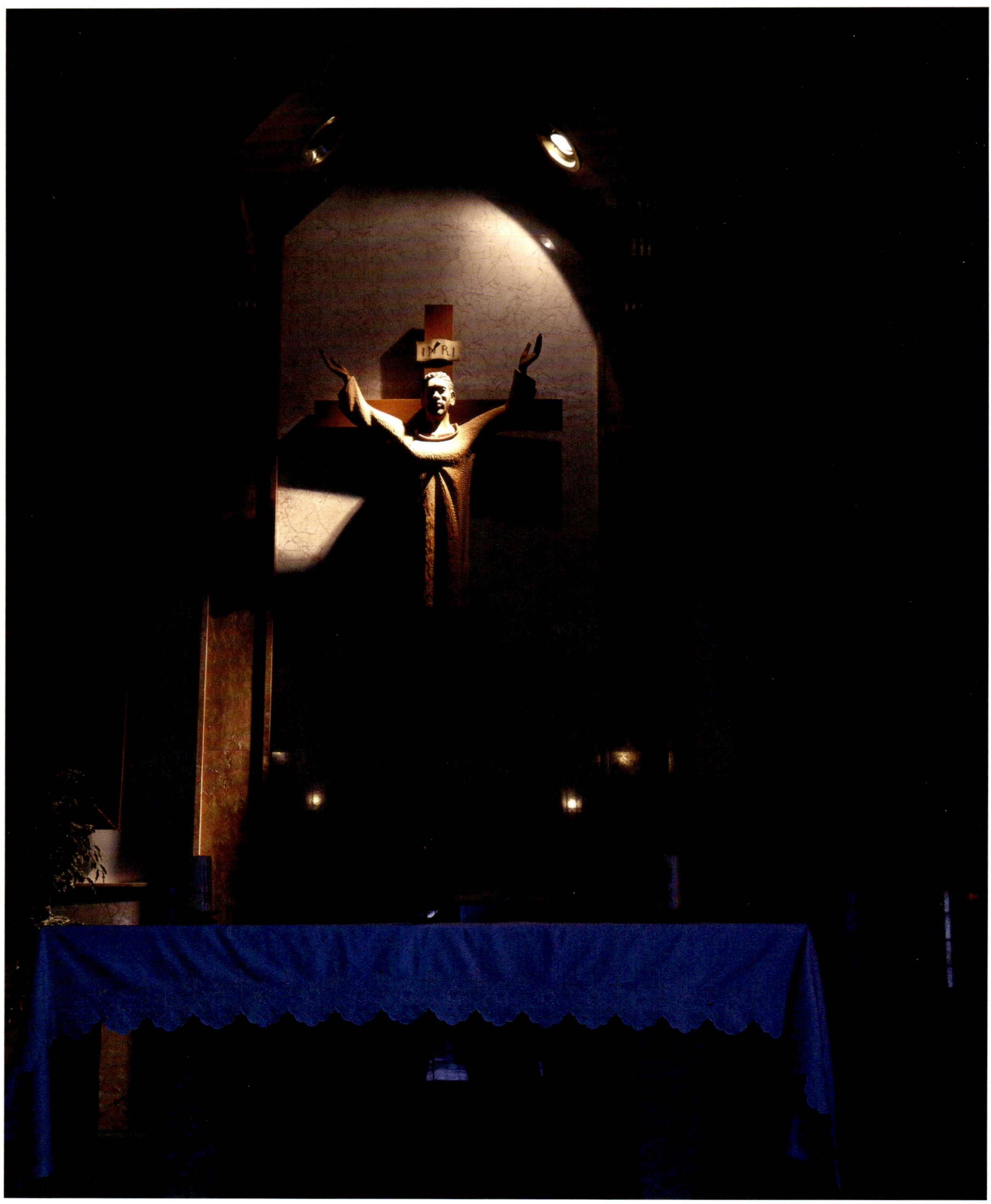

INRI

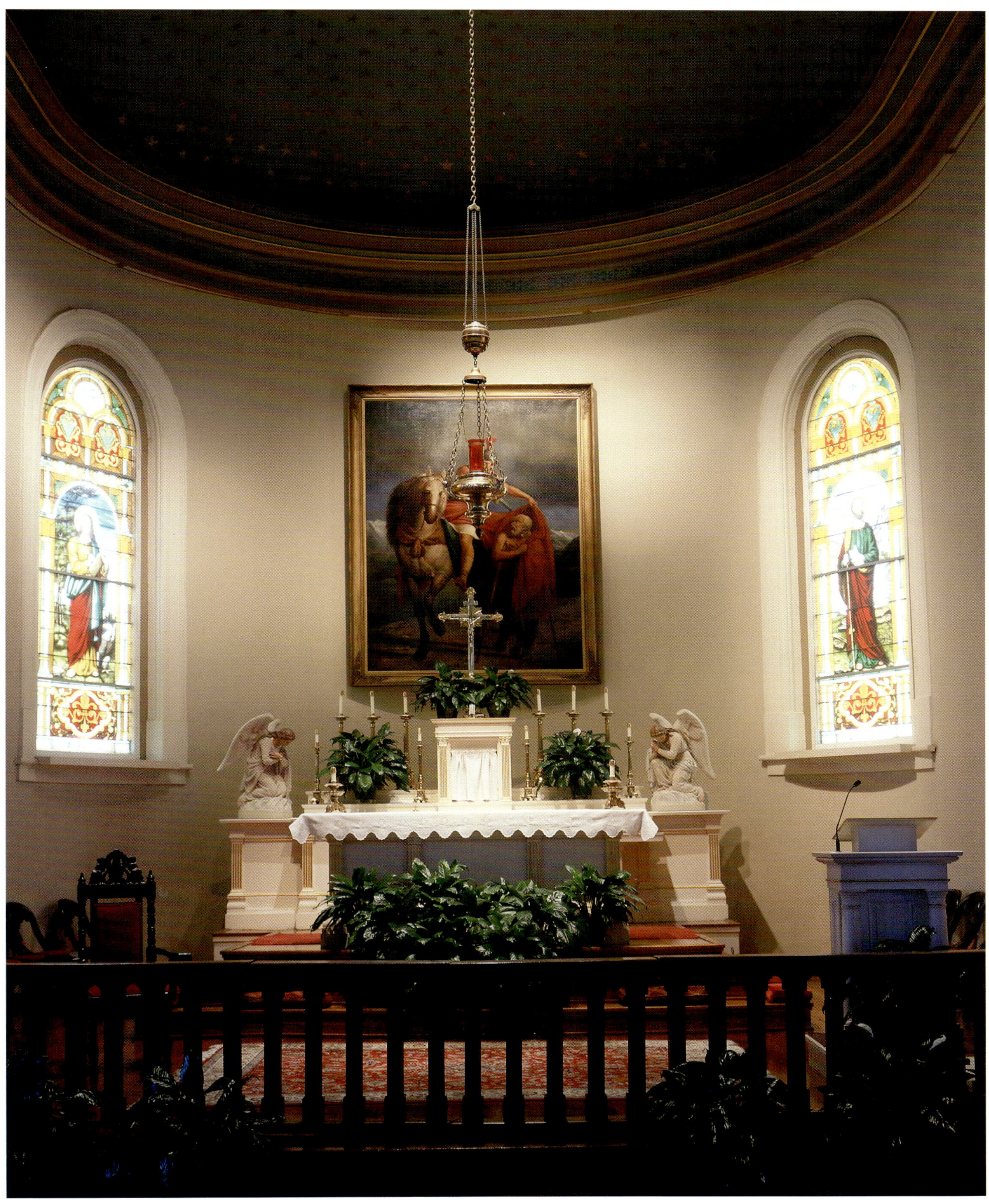

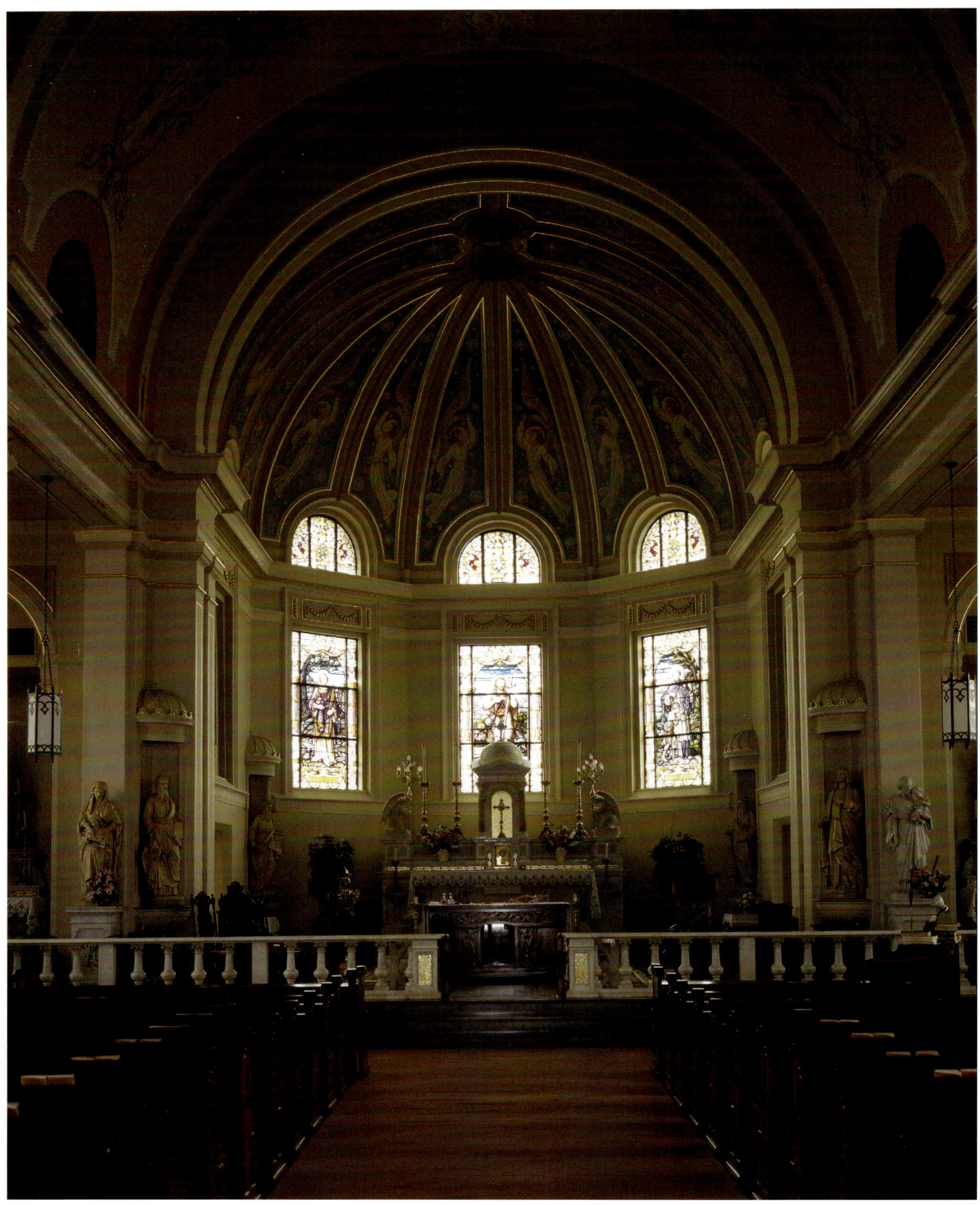

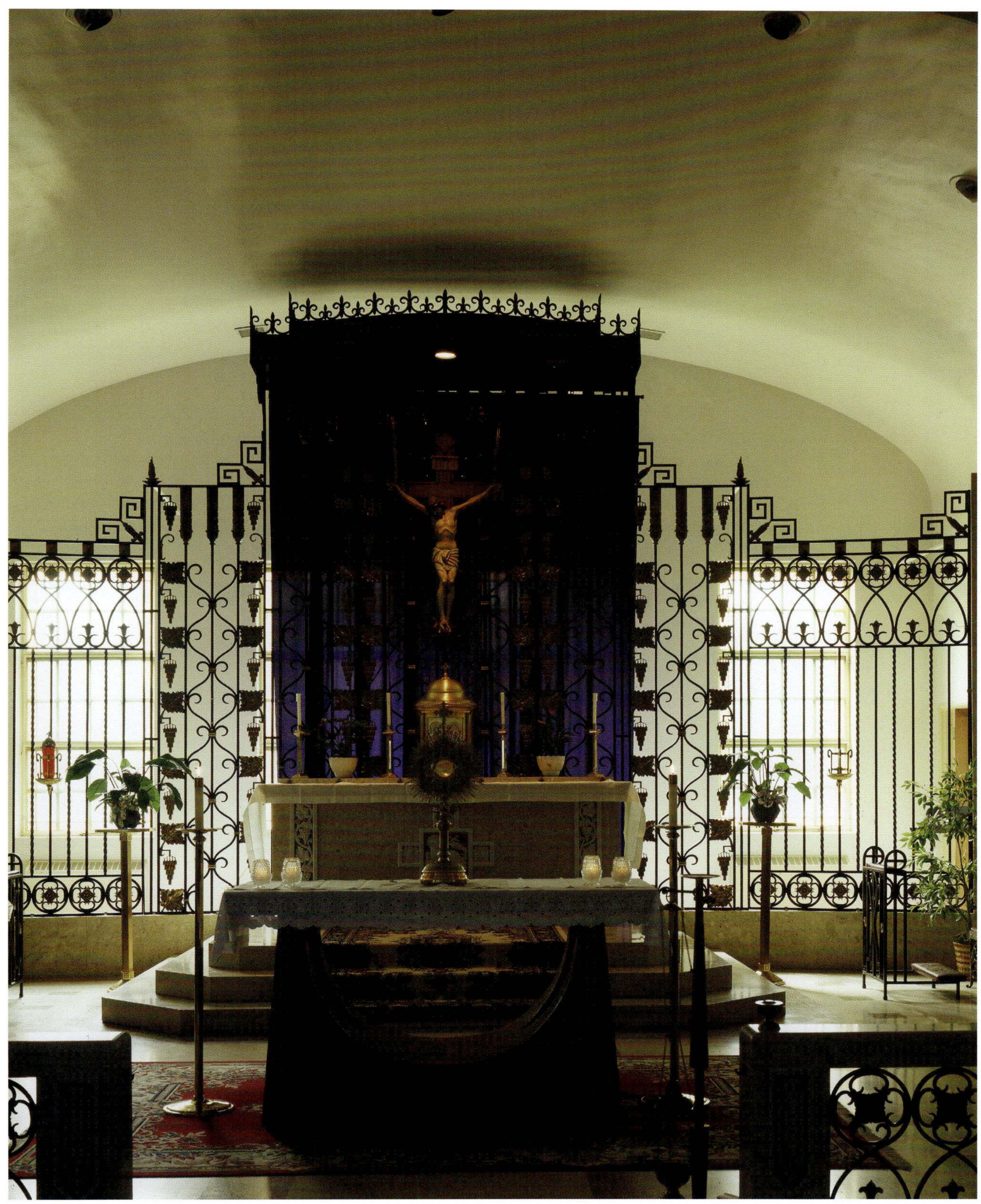

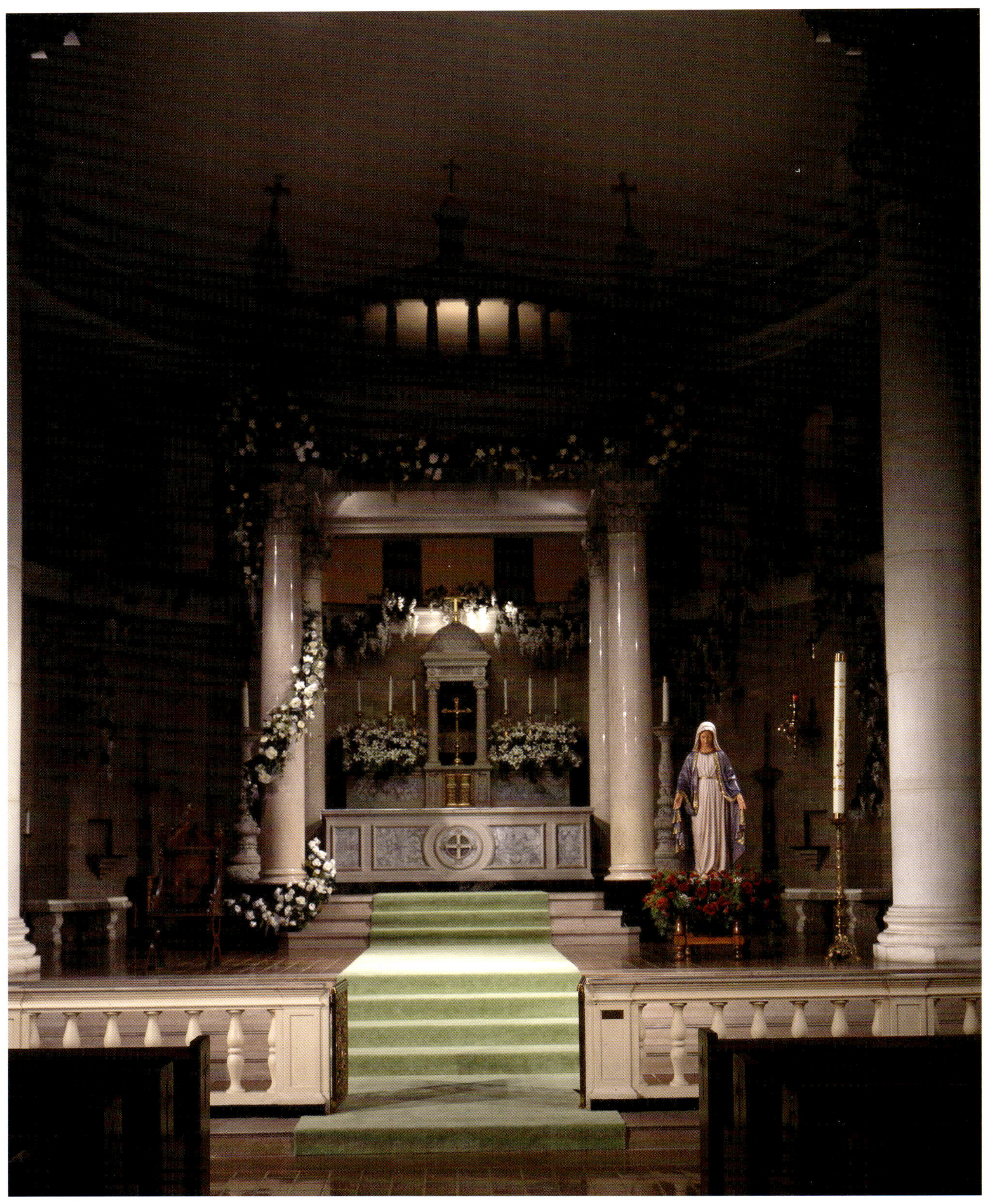

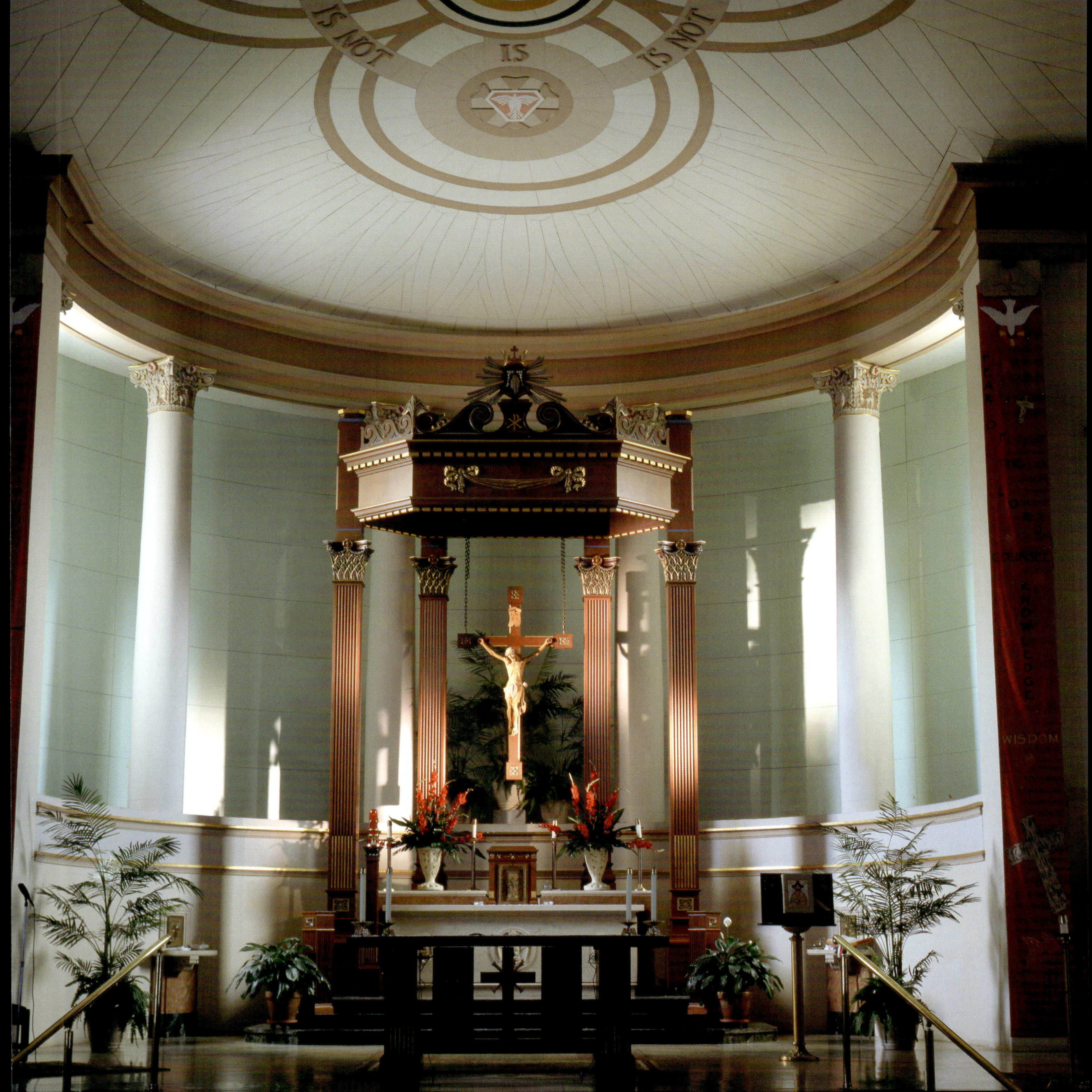

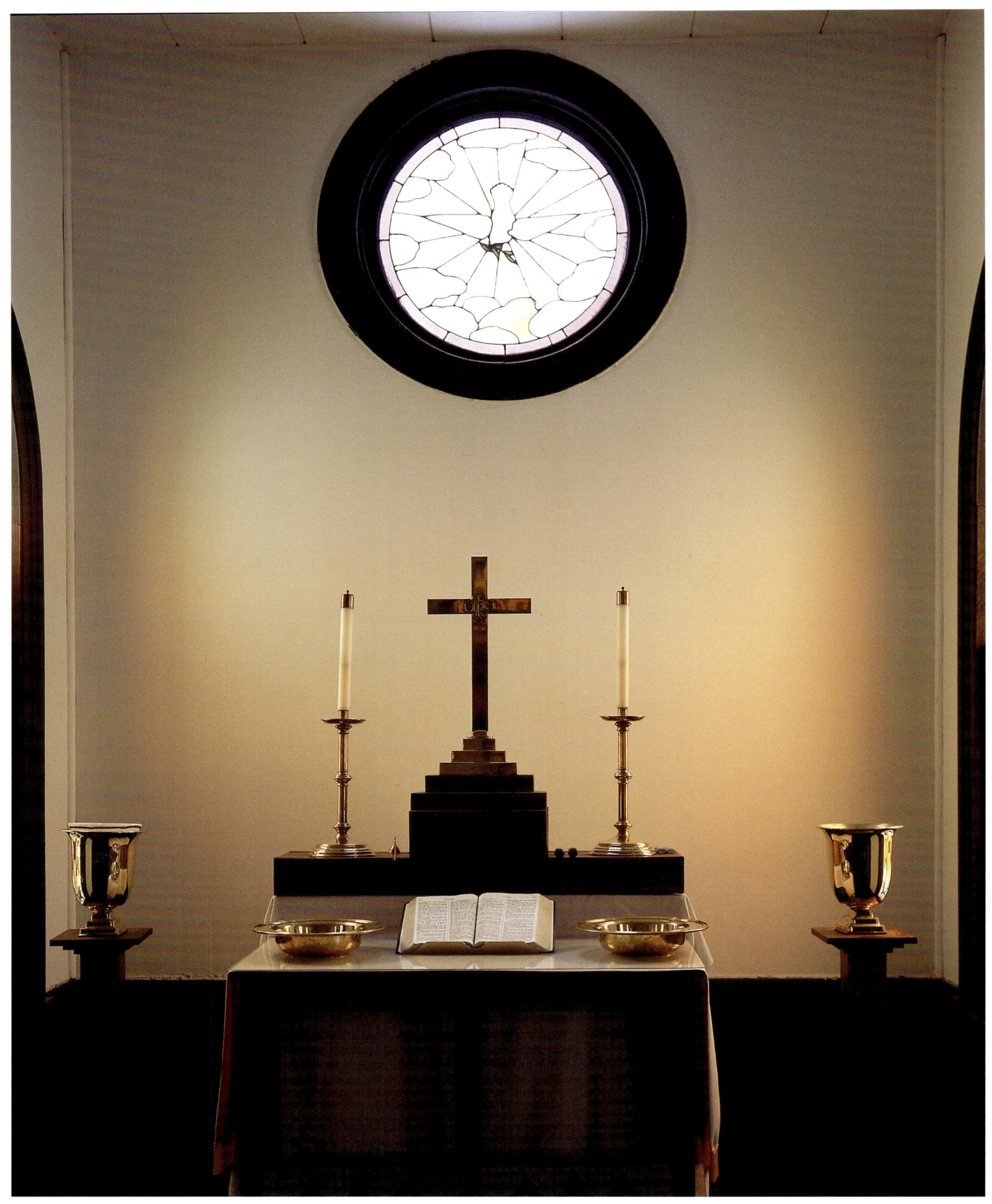

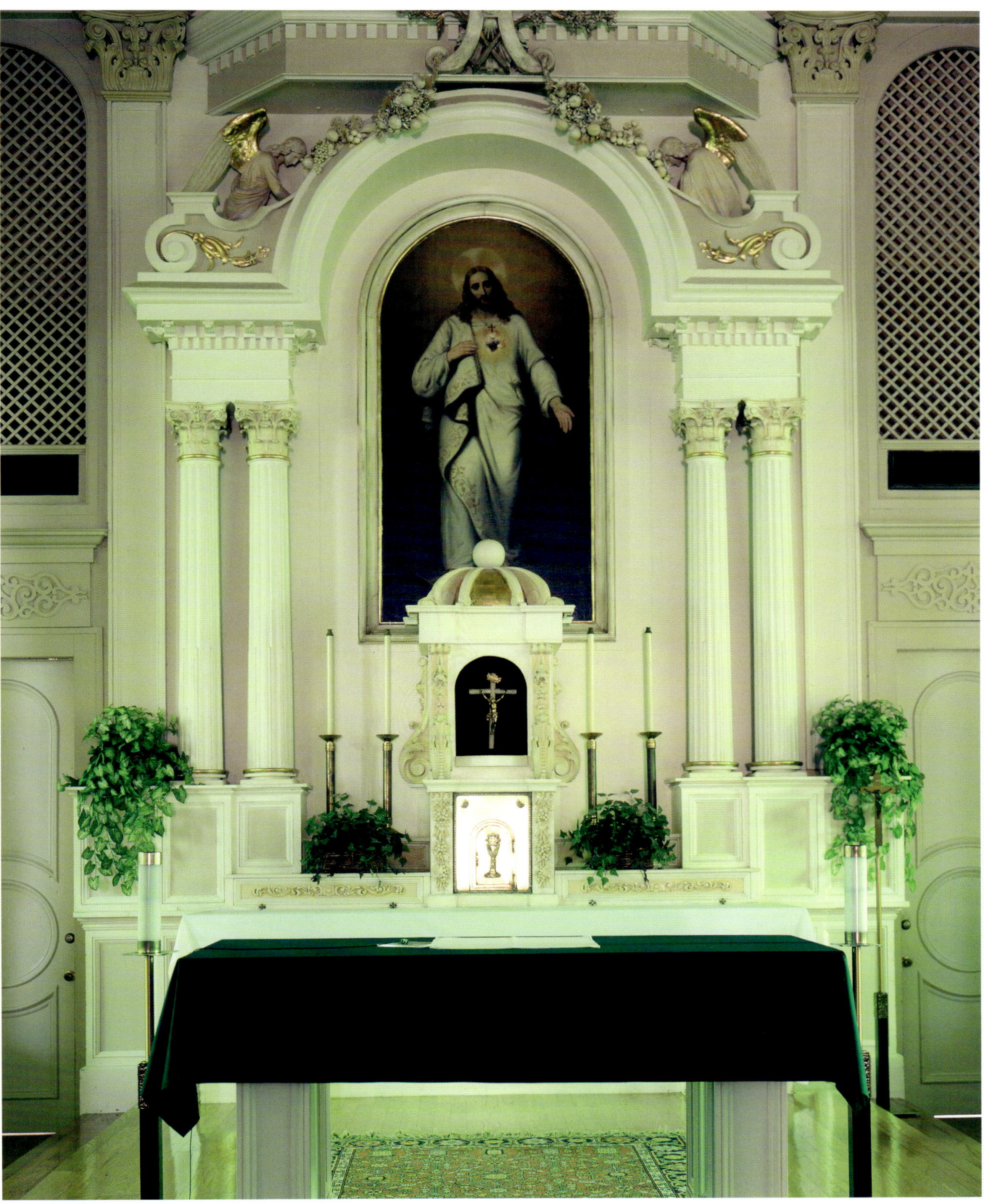

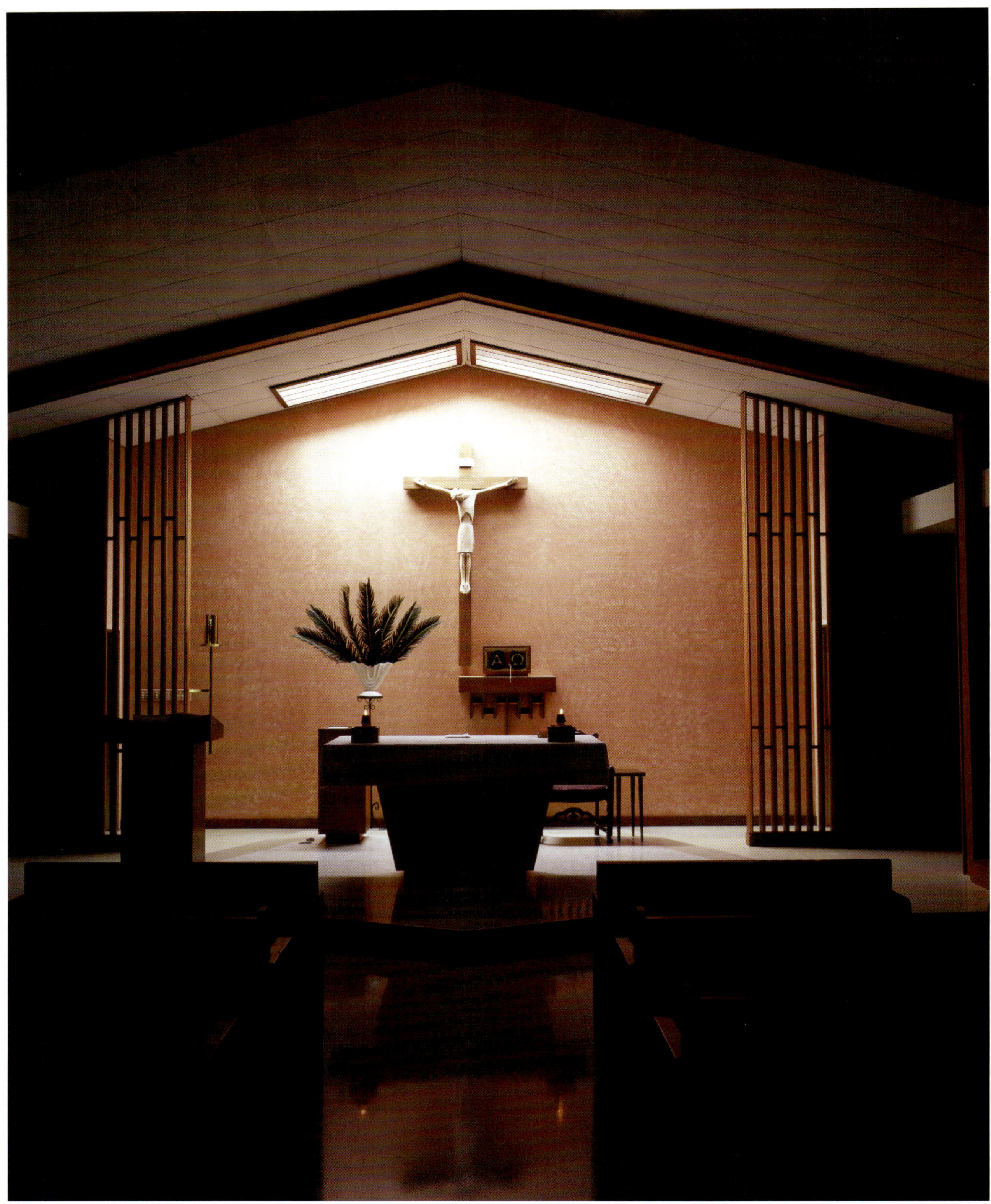

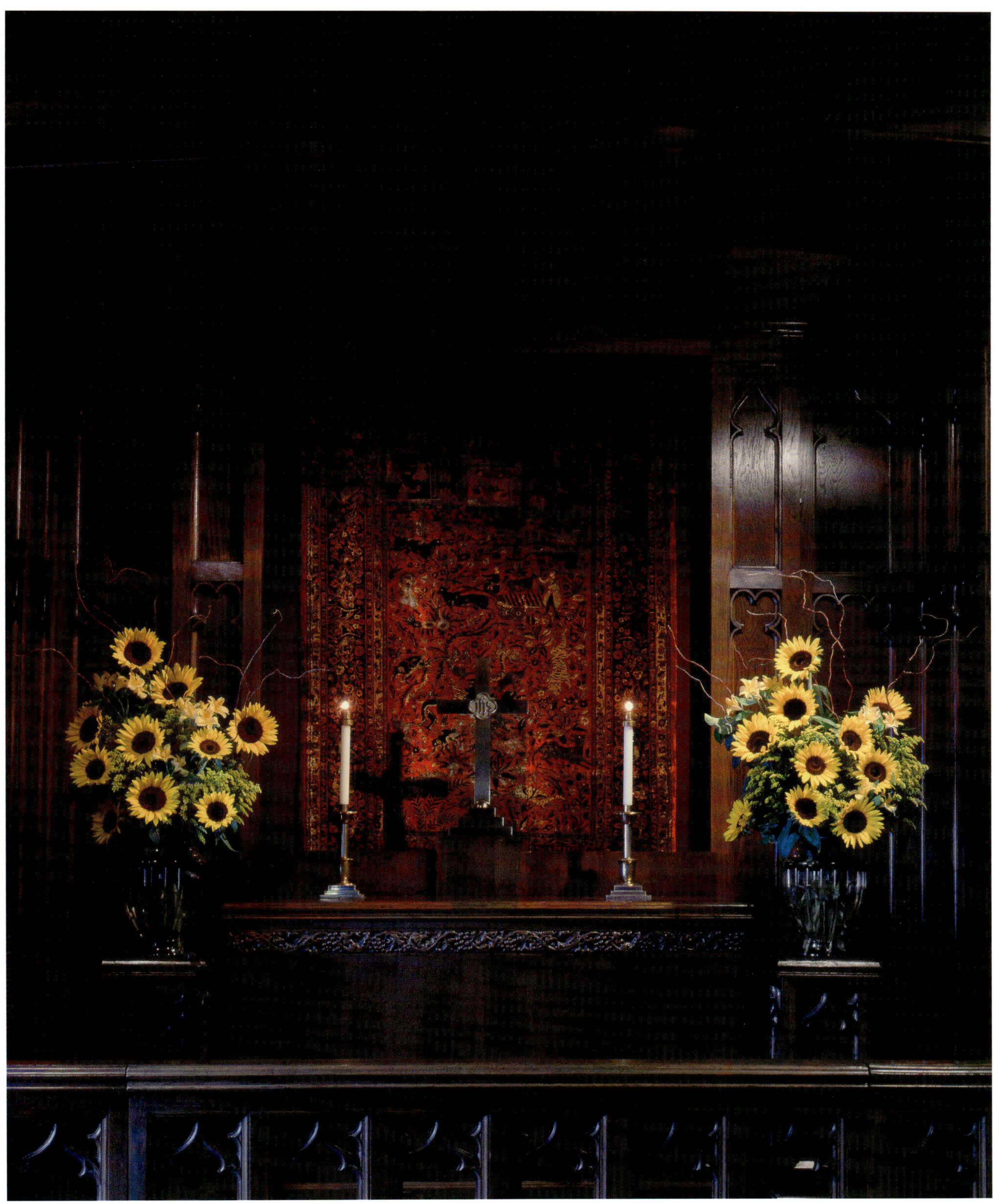

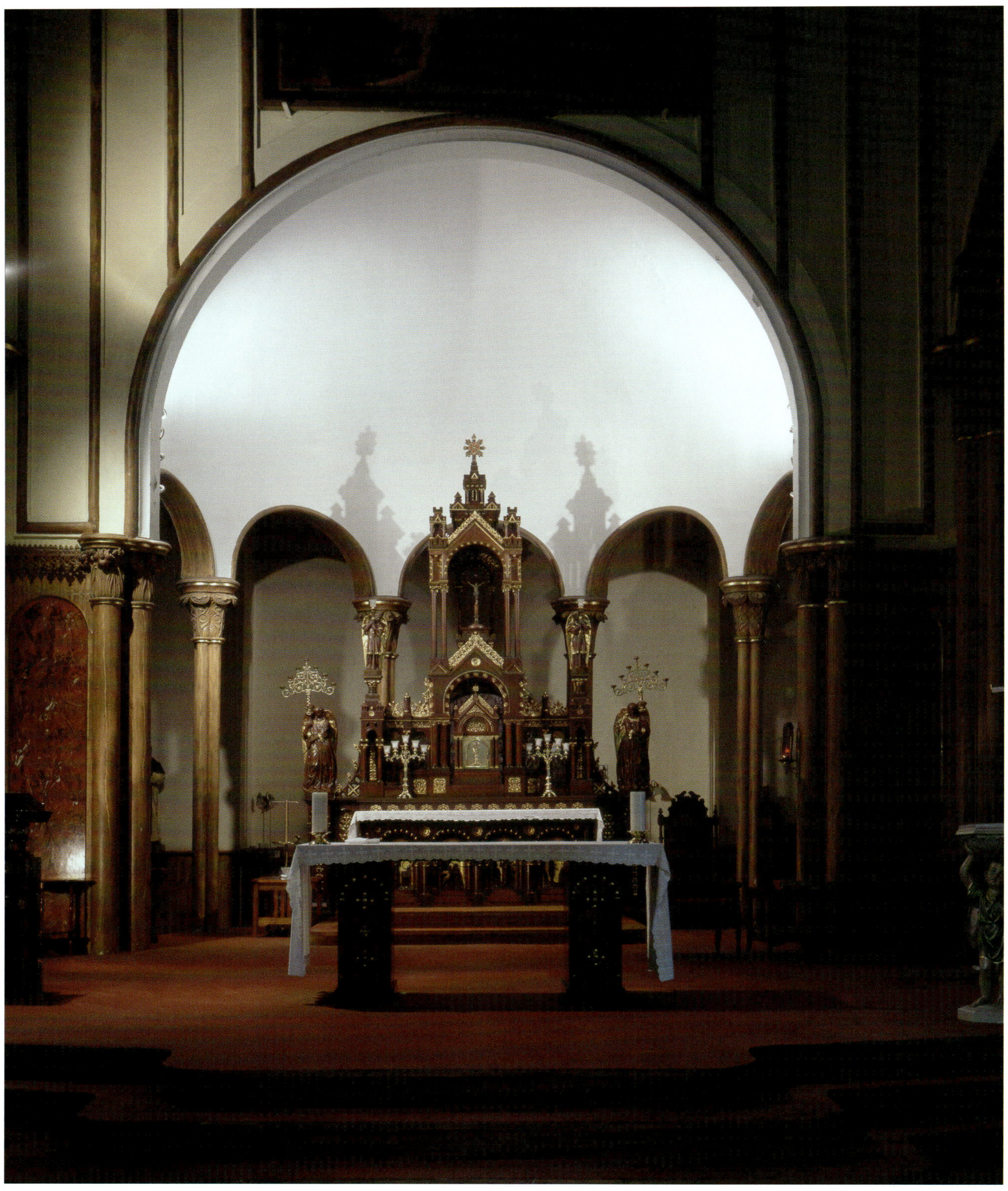

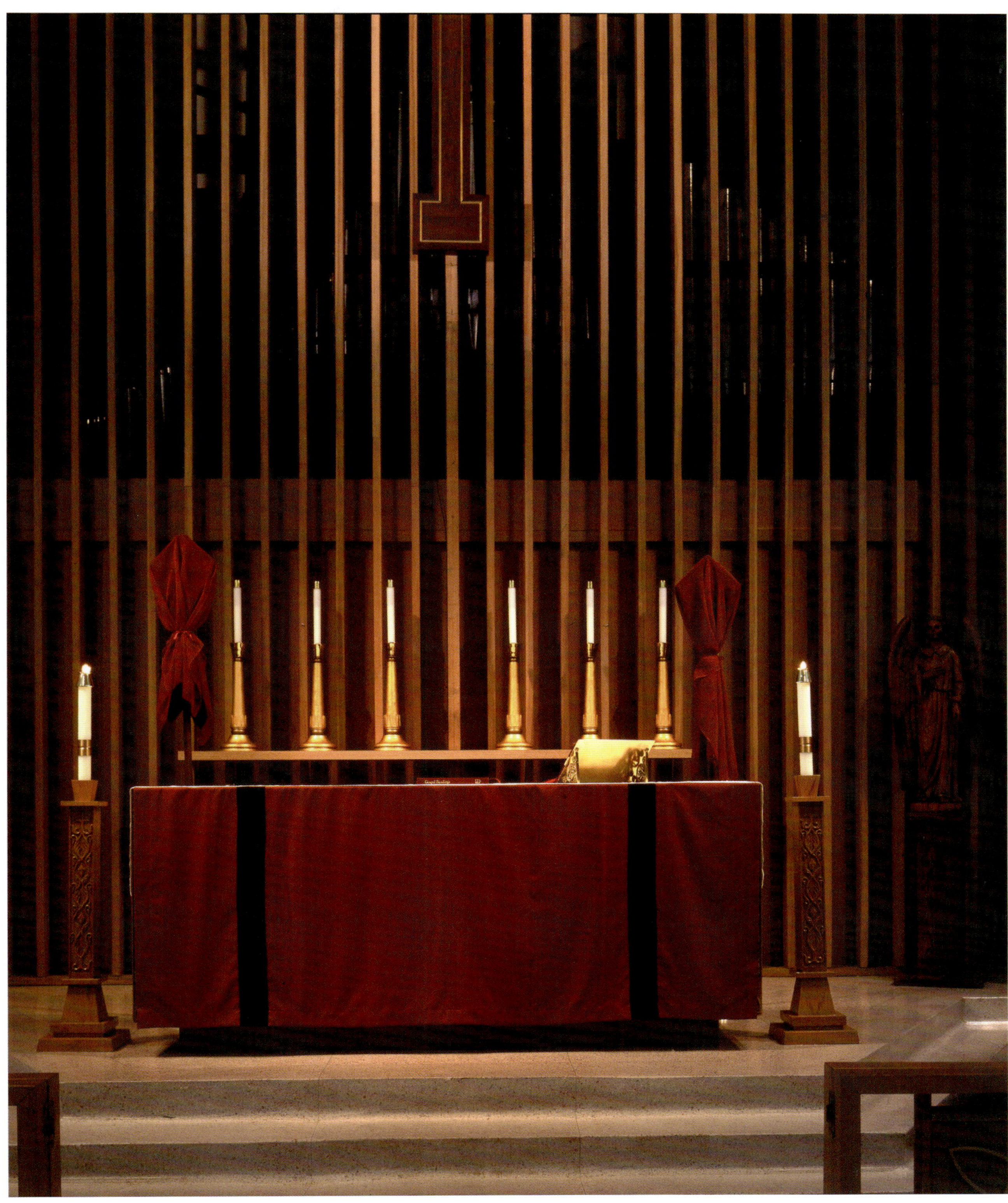

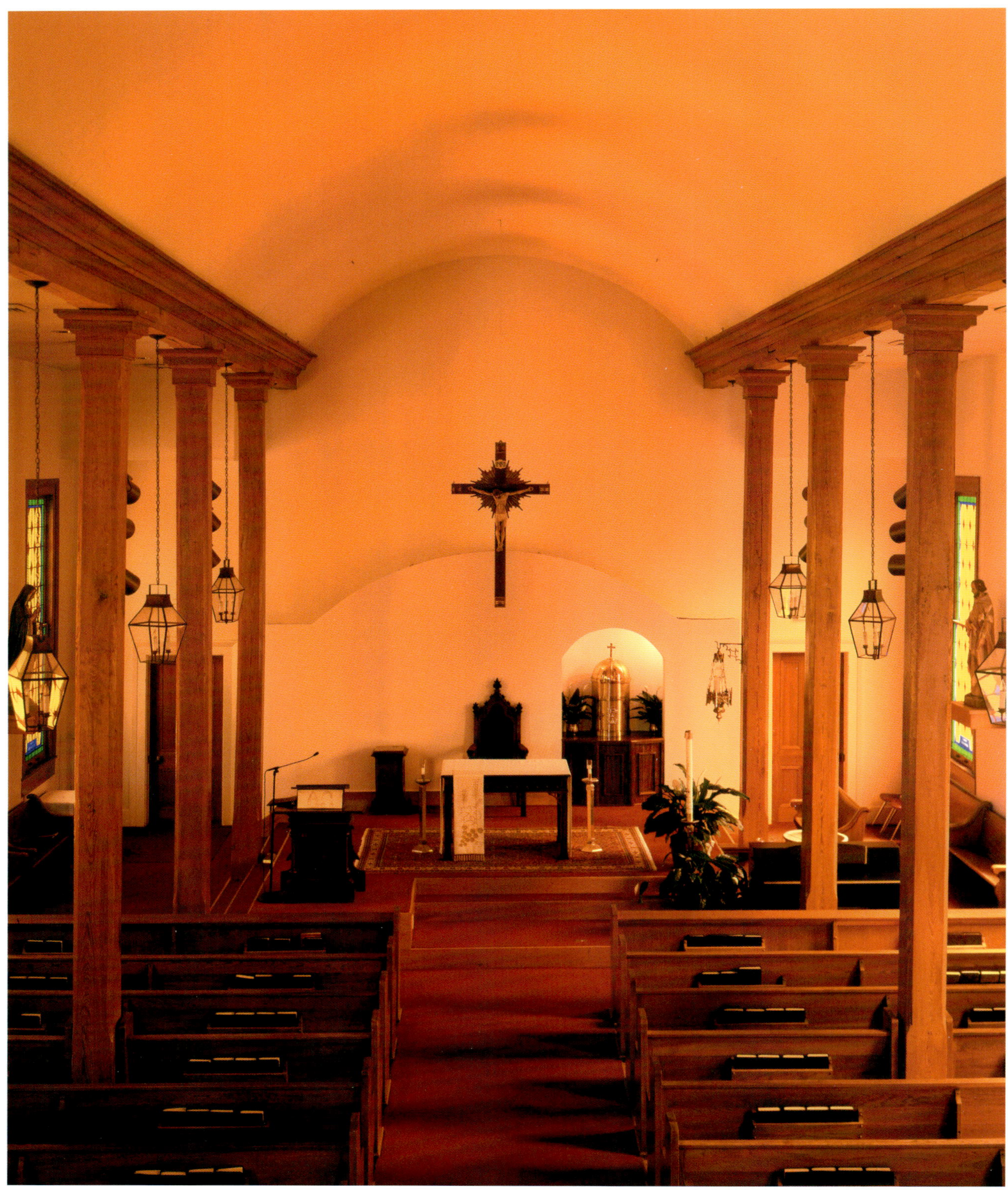

Angels, Deities, Madonnas, and Saints

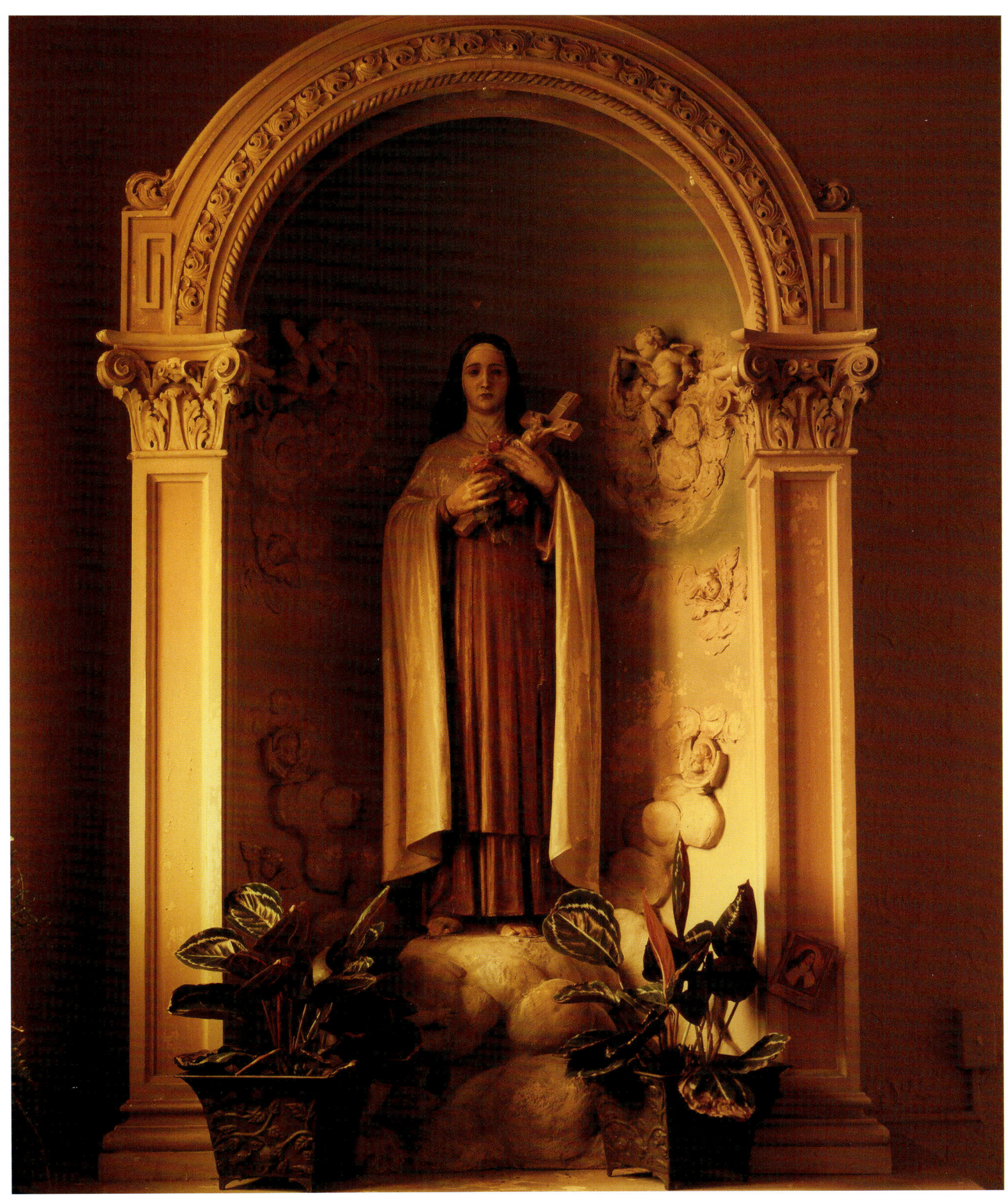

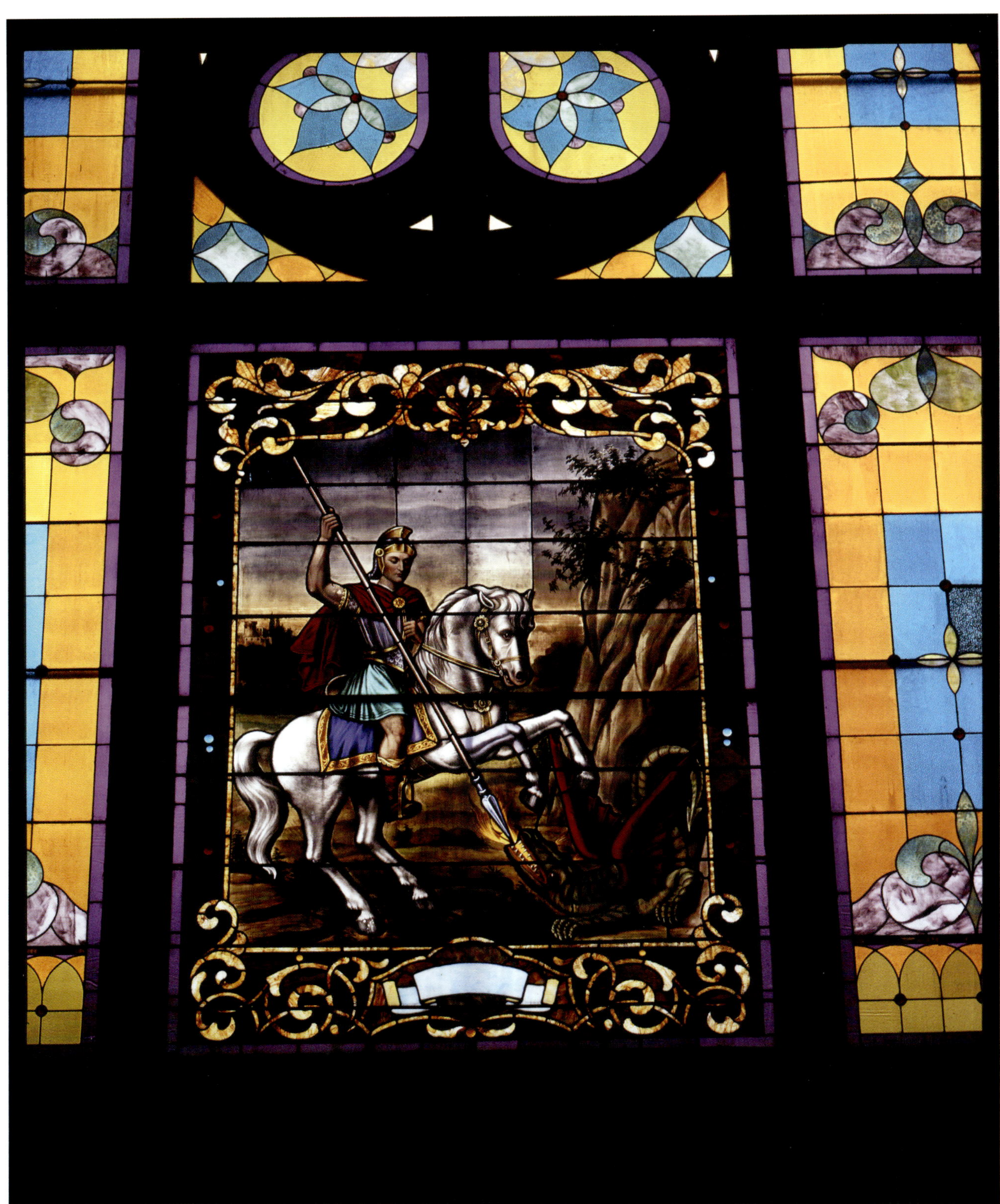

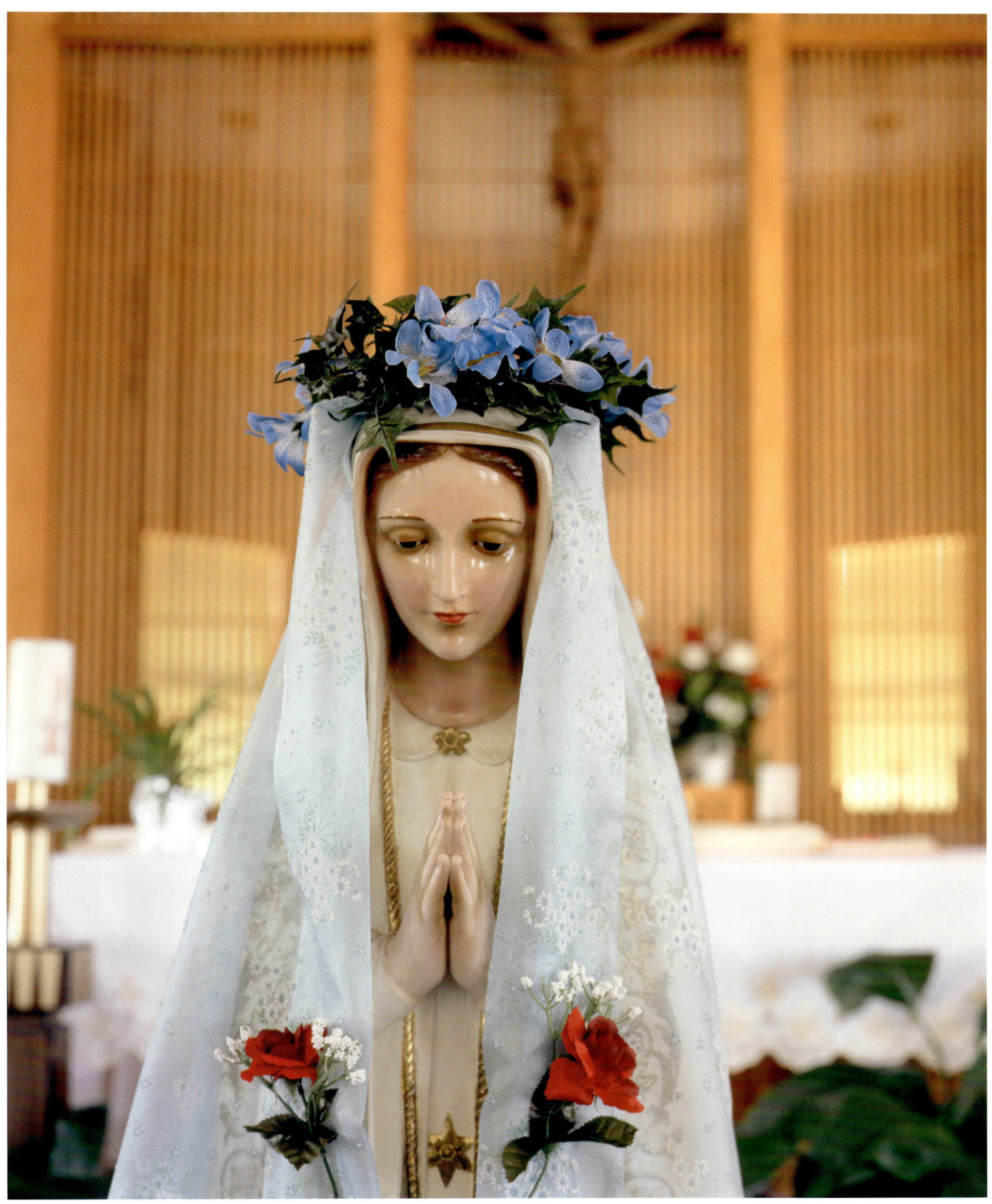

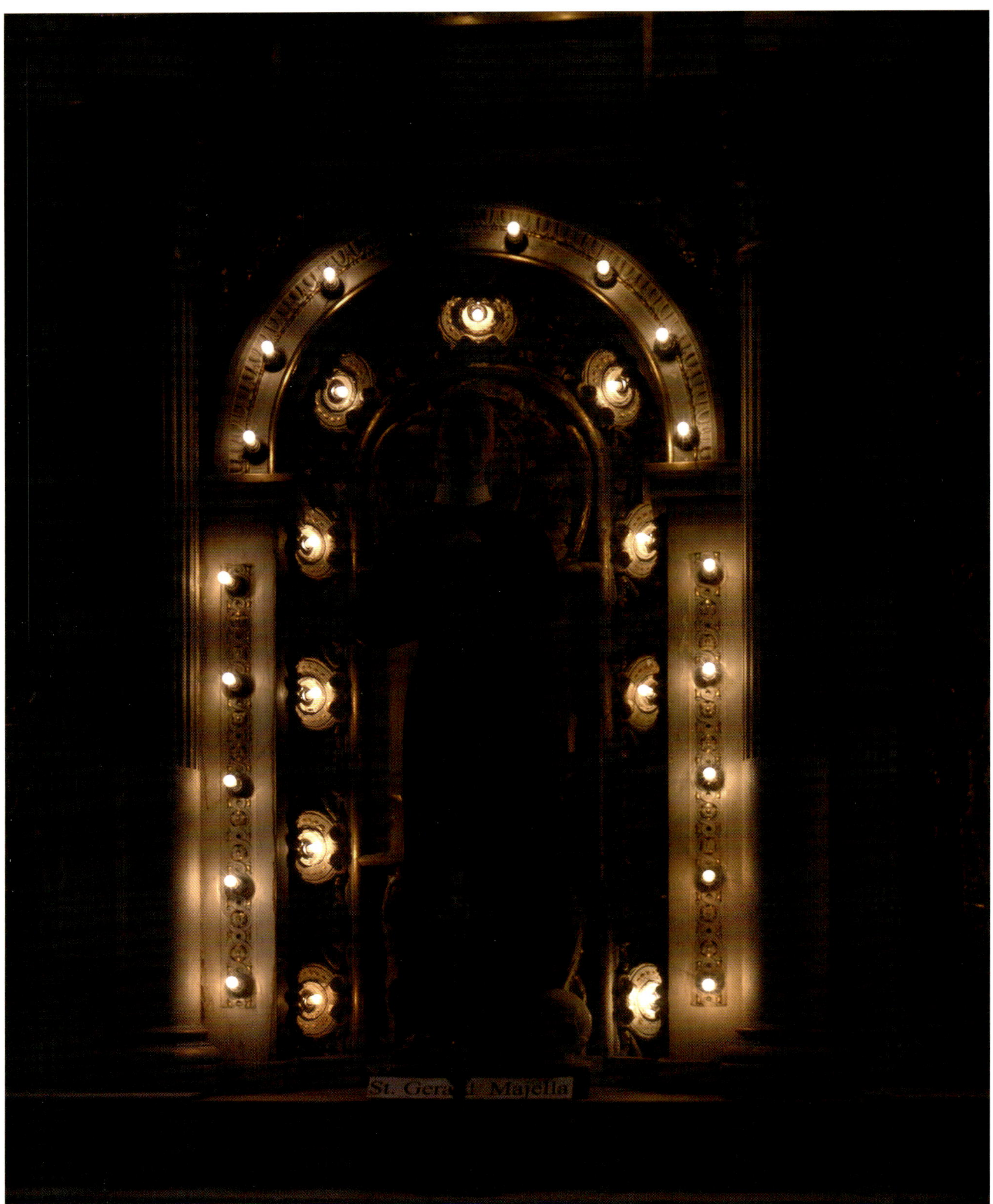
St. Gerard Majella

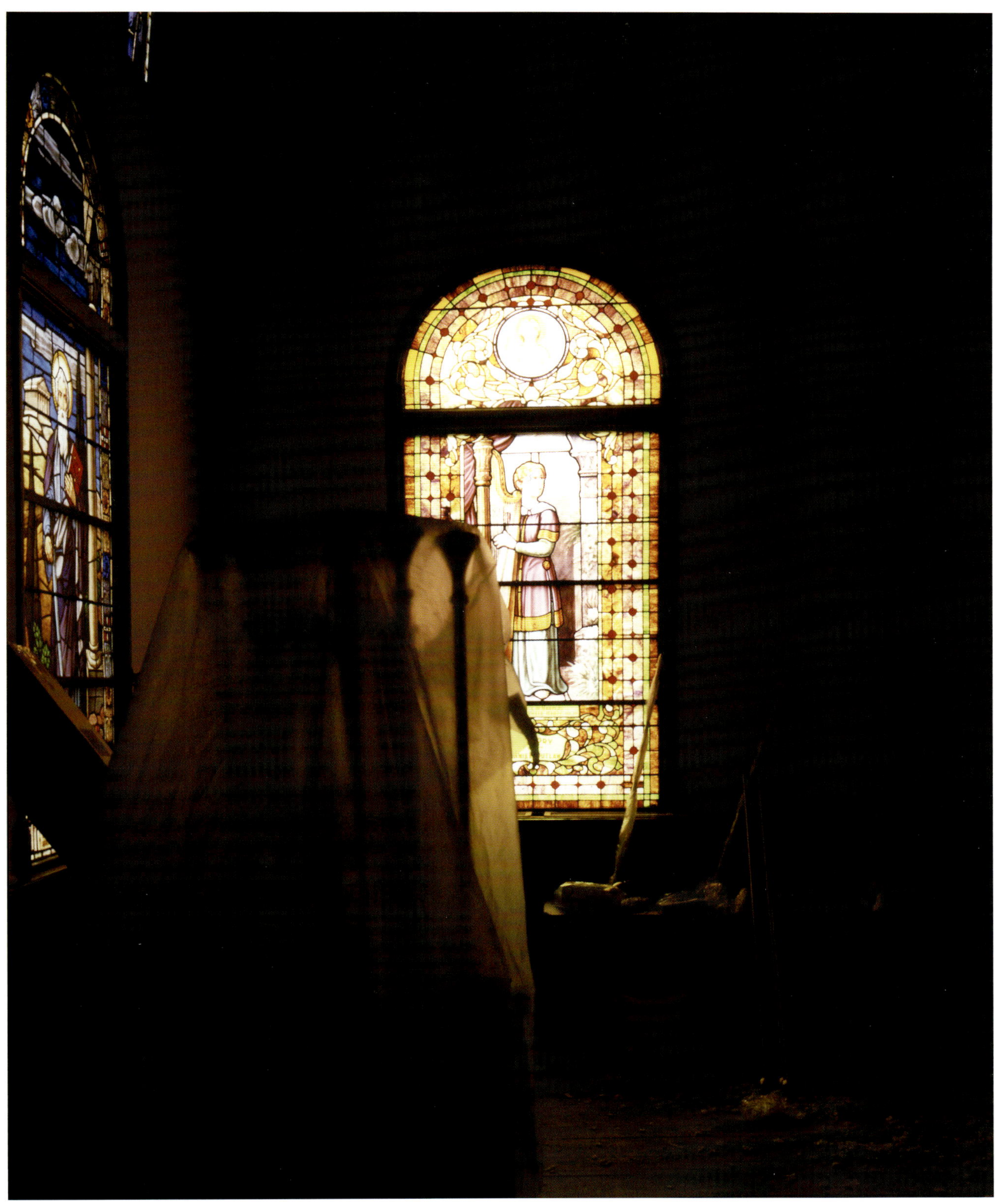

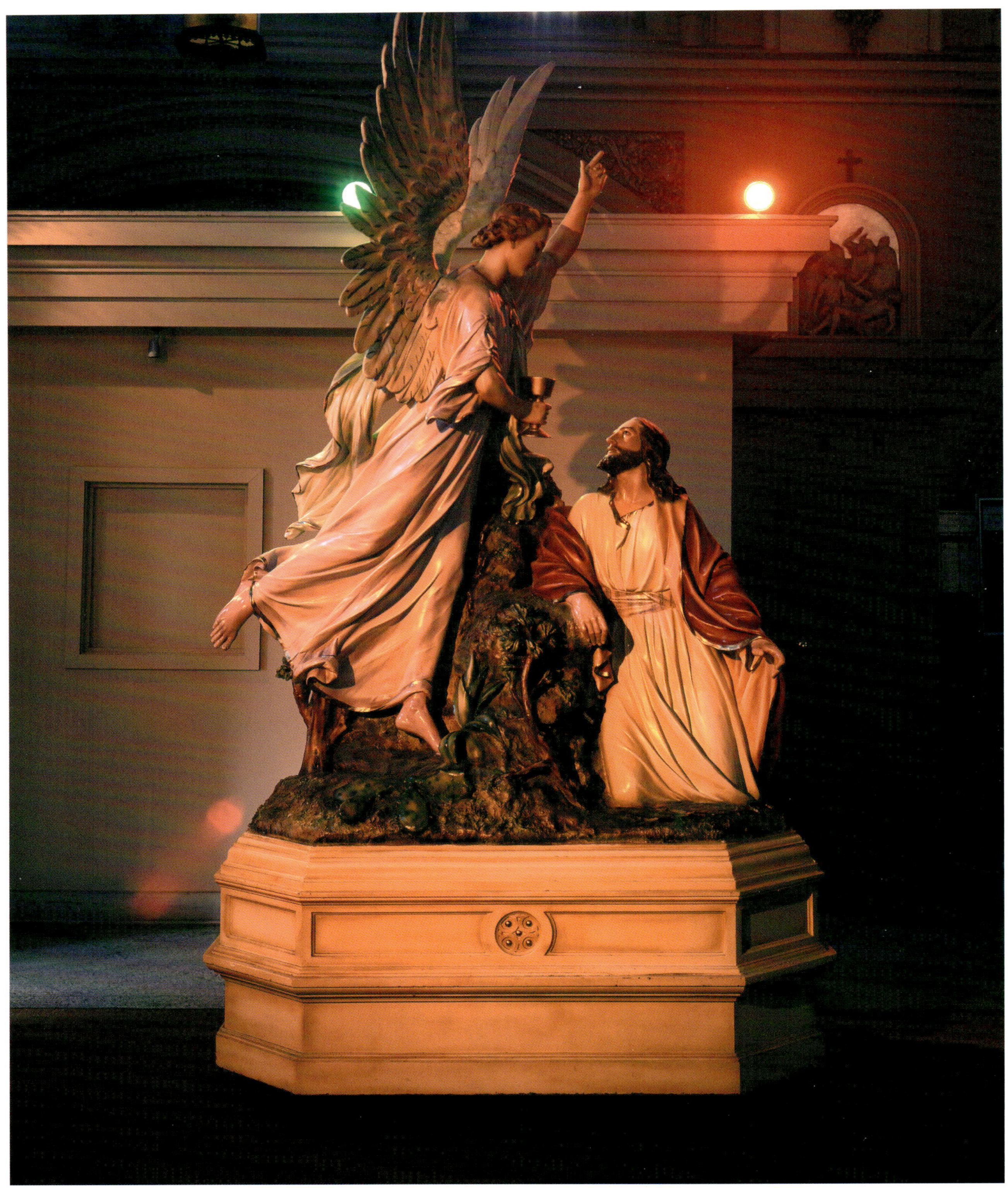

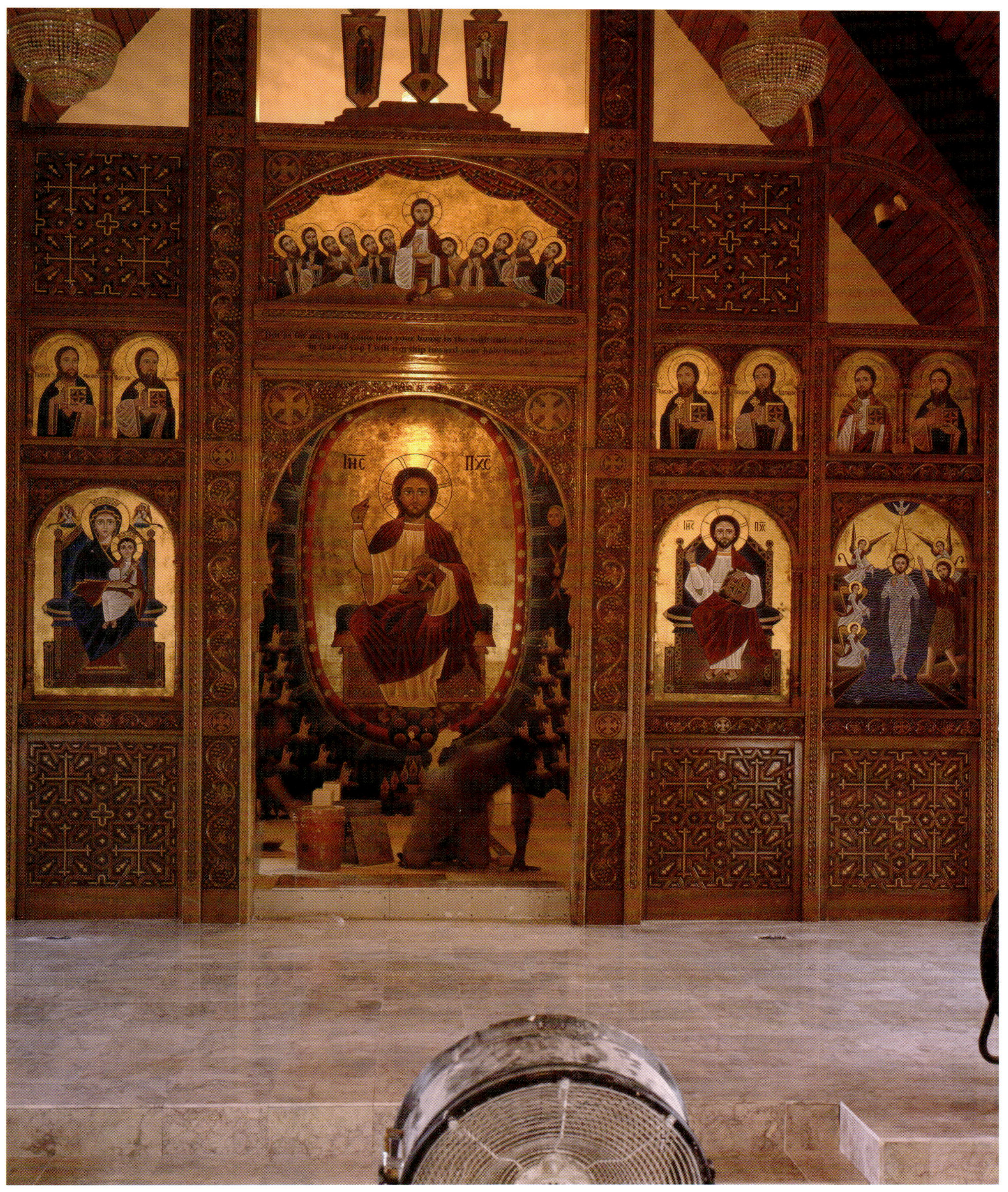

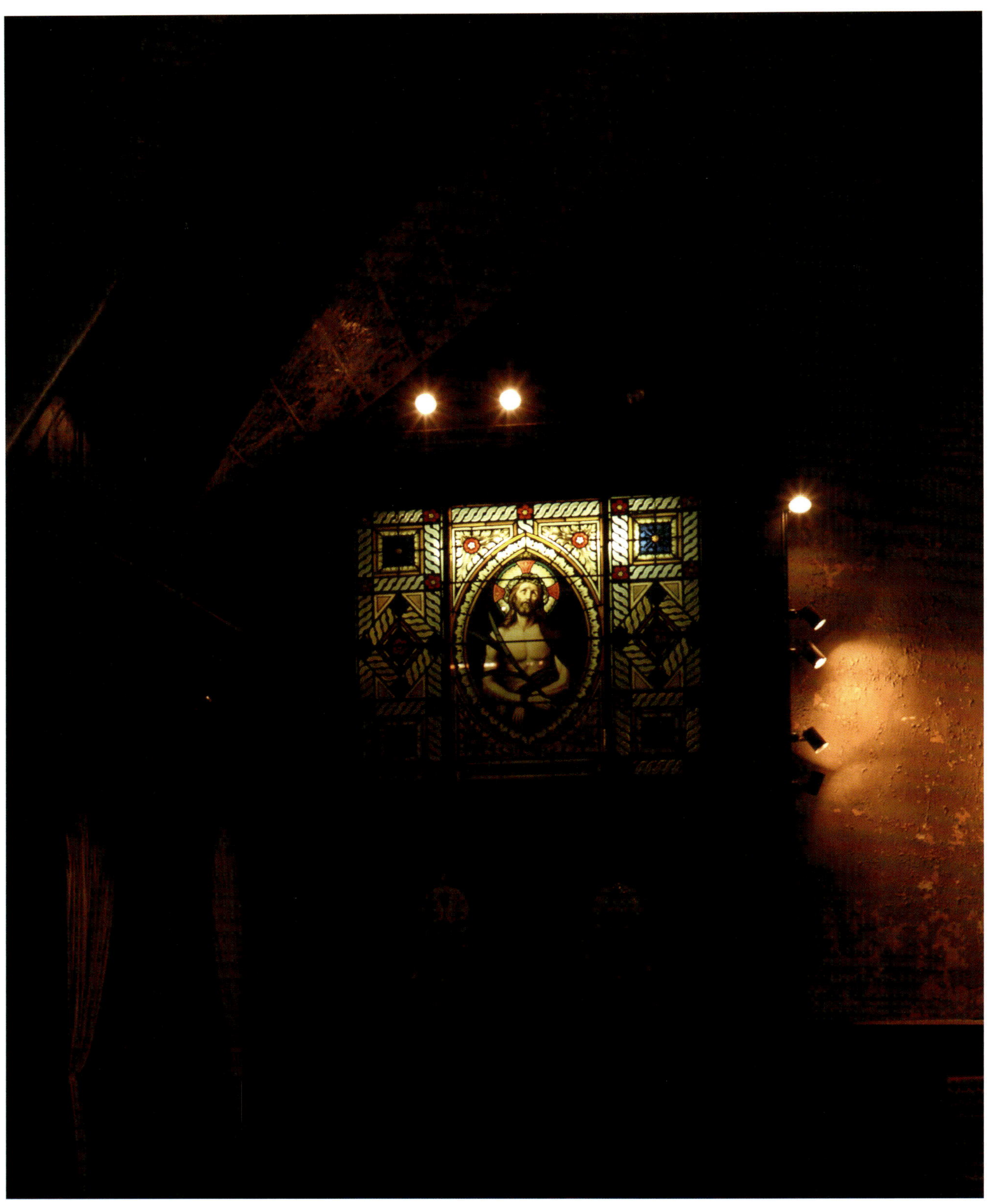

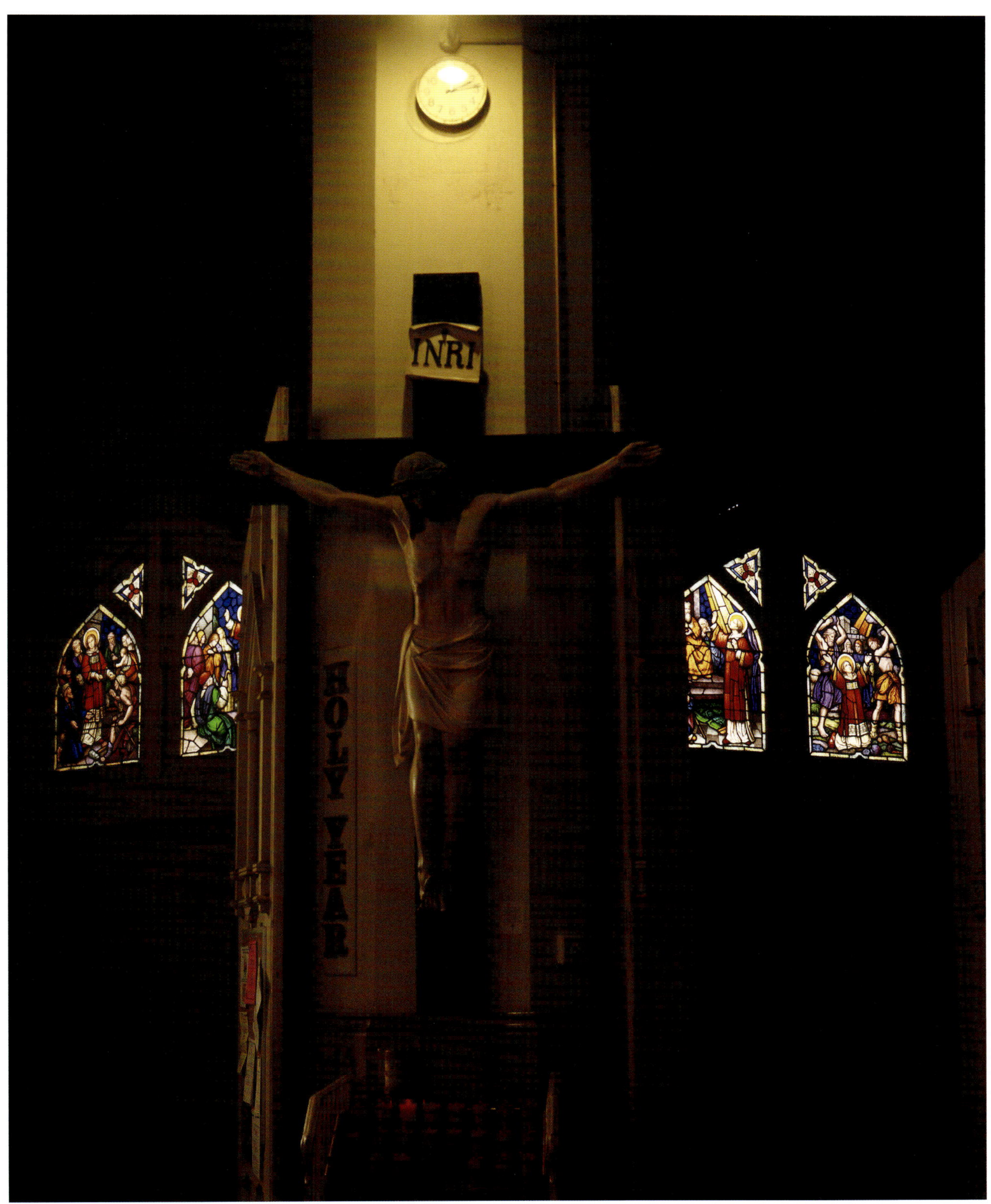
INRI
HOLY YEAR

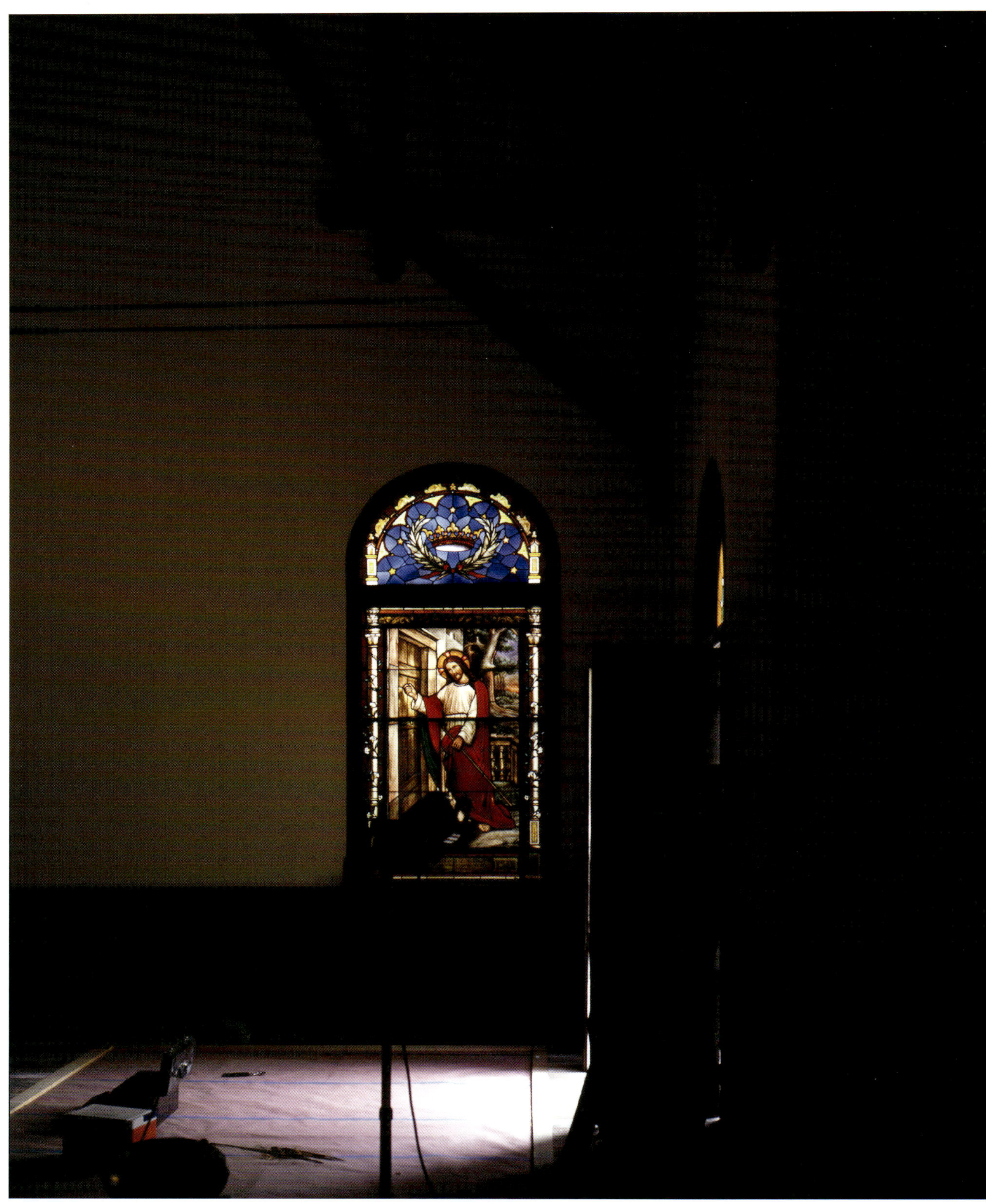

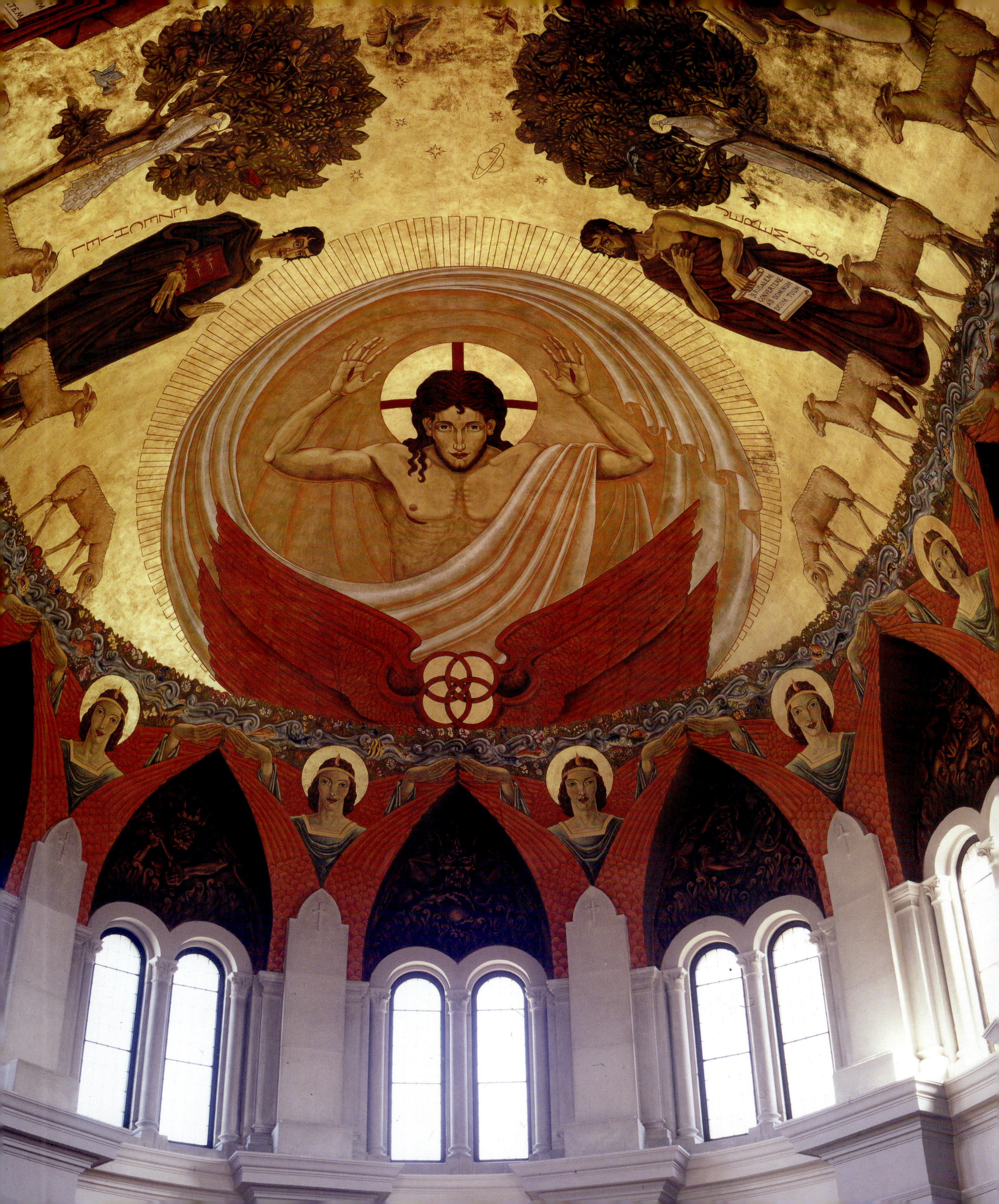

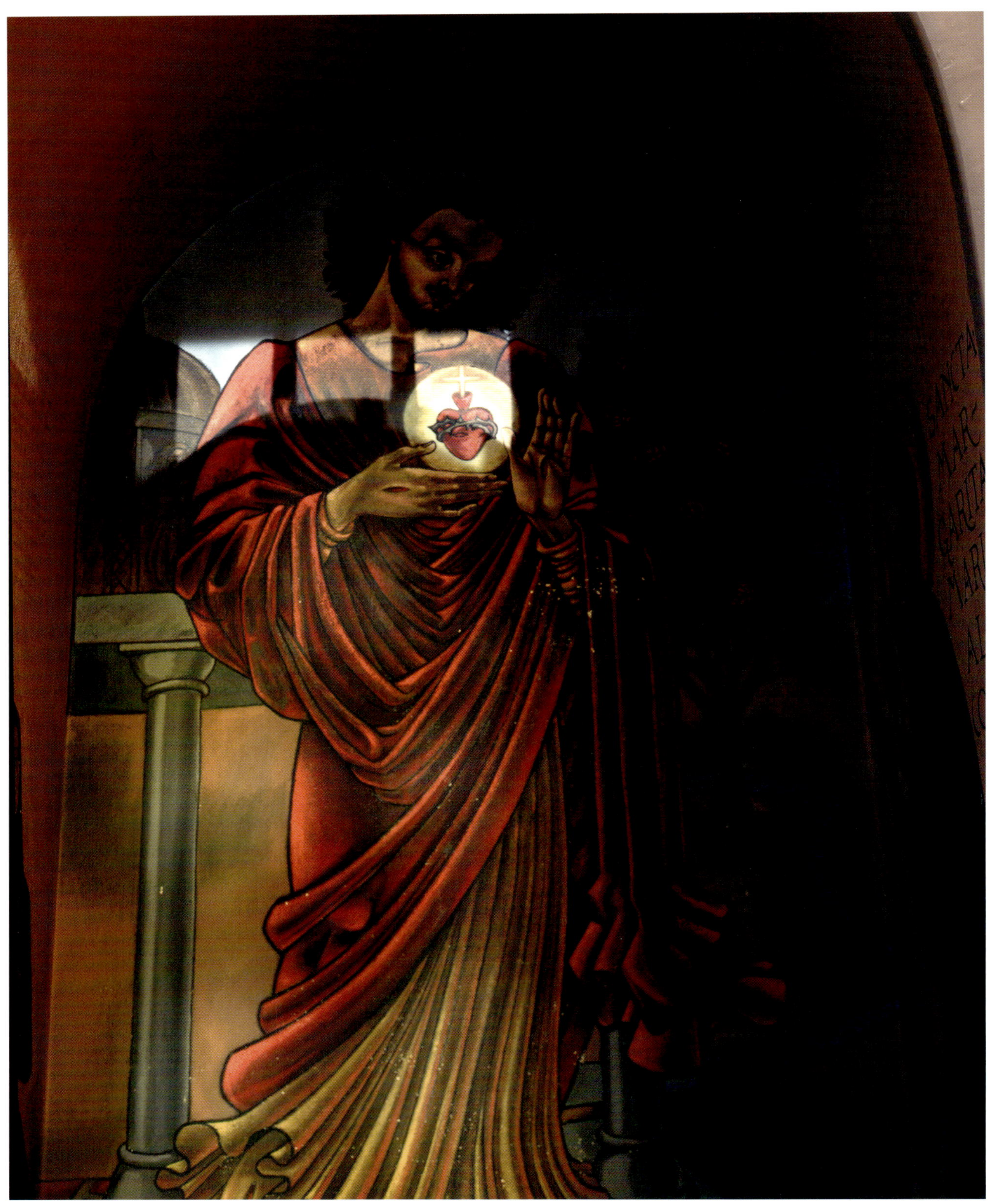

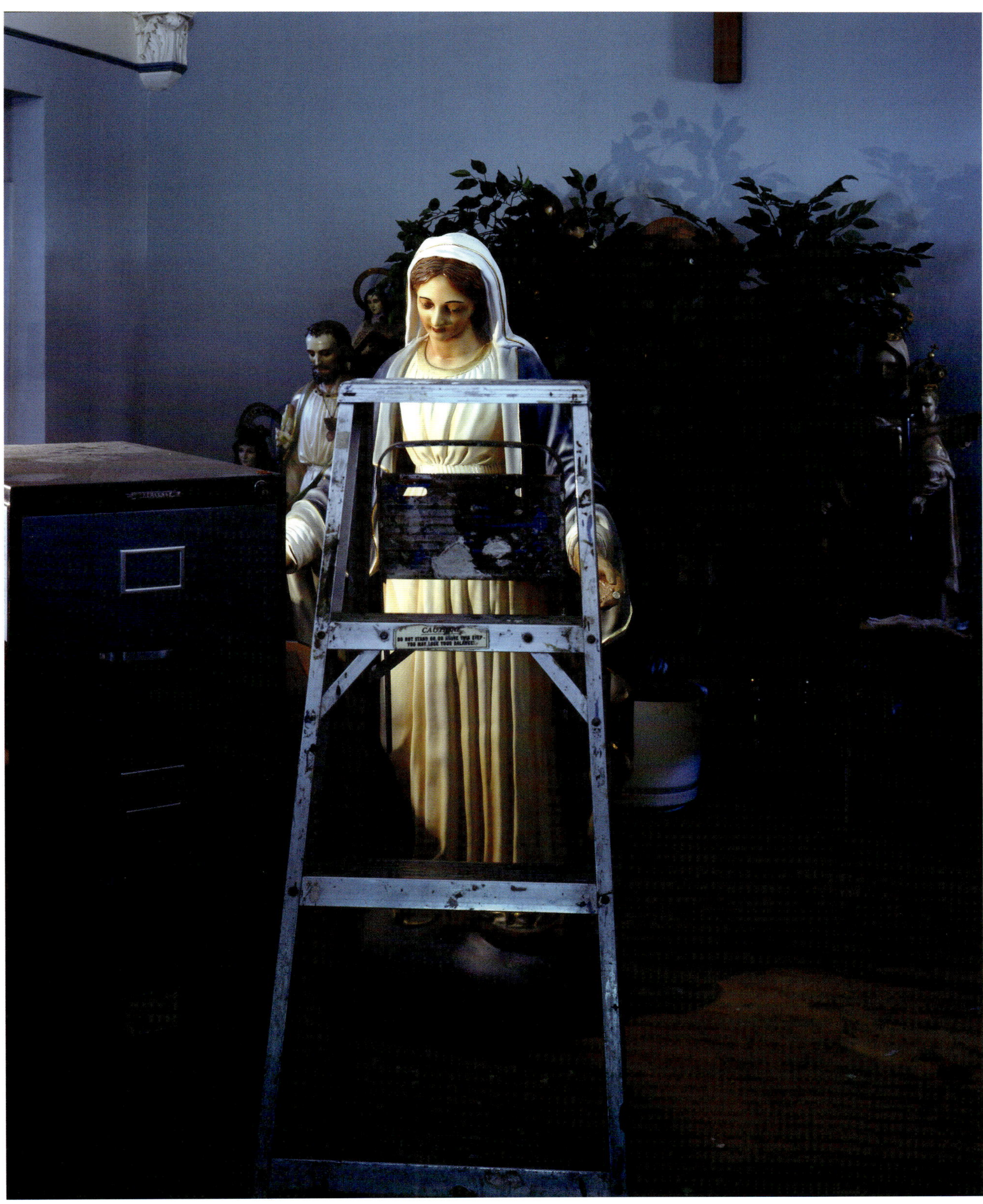
CAUTION
DO NOT STAND ON OR ABOVE THIS STEP
YOU MAY LOSE YOUR BALANCE

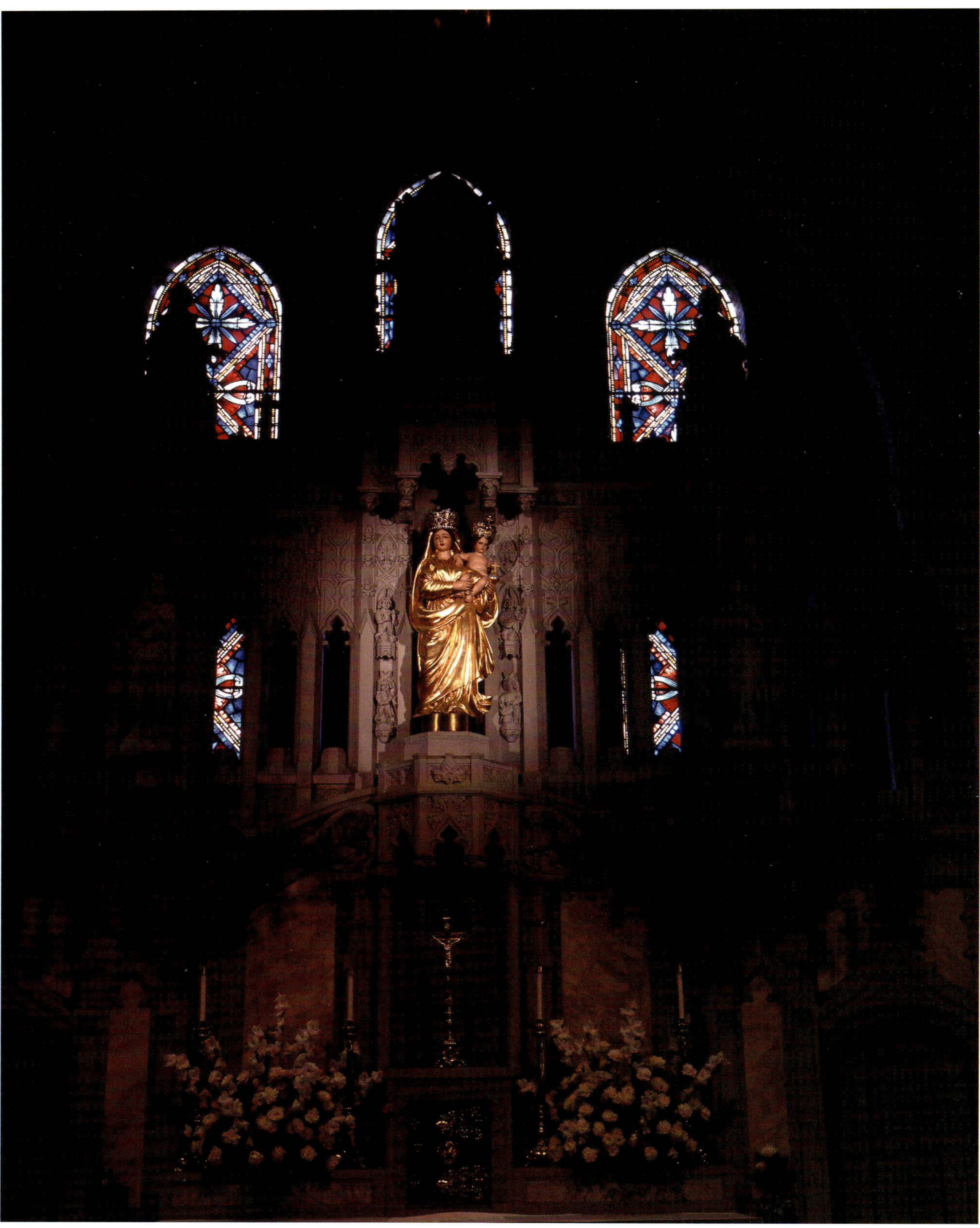

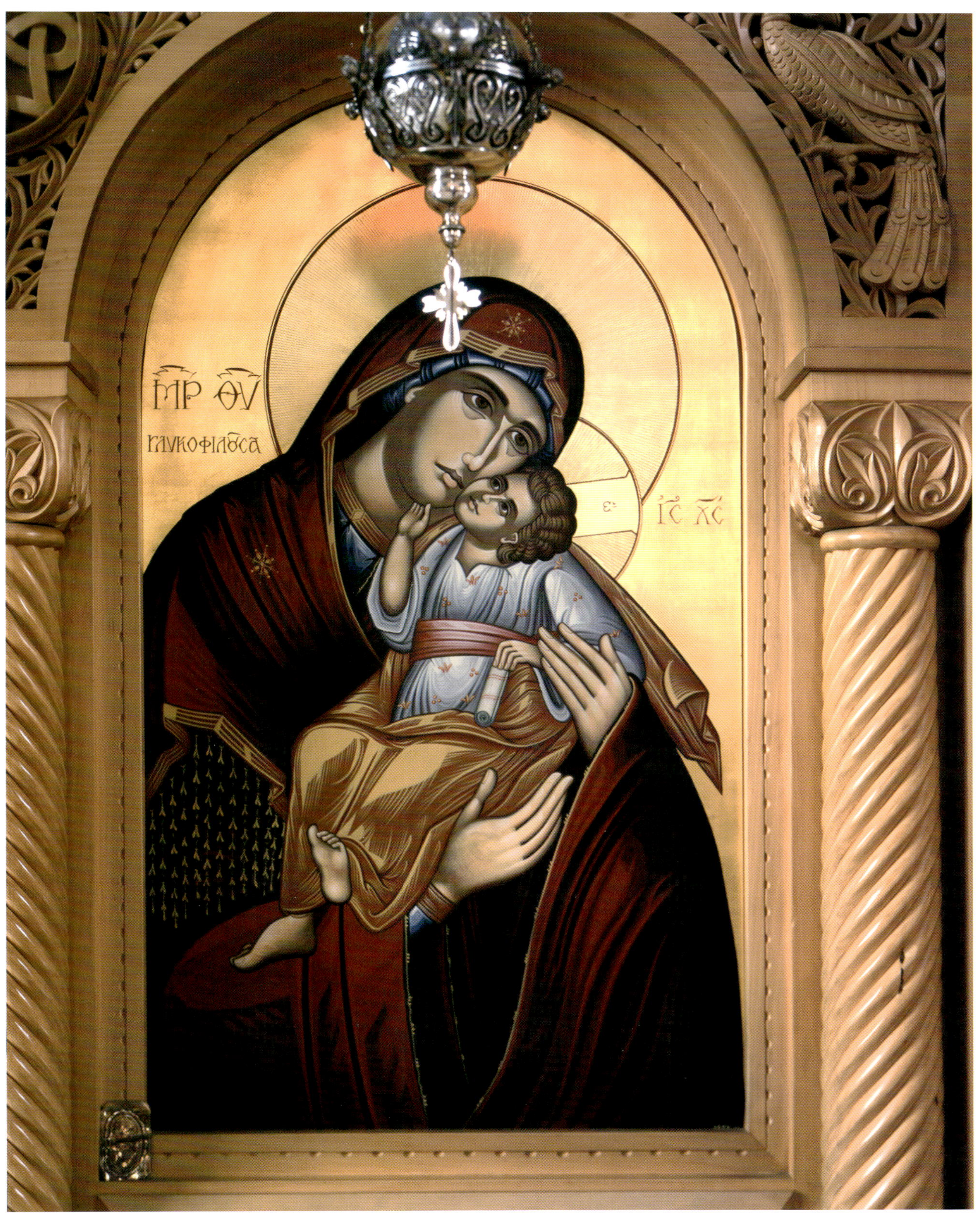

ΜΡ ΘΥ
ΓΛΥΚΟΦΙΛΟΥΣΑ
ΙϹ ΧϹ

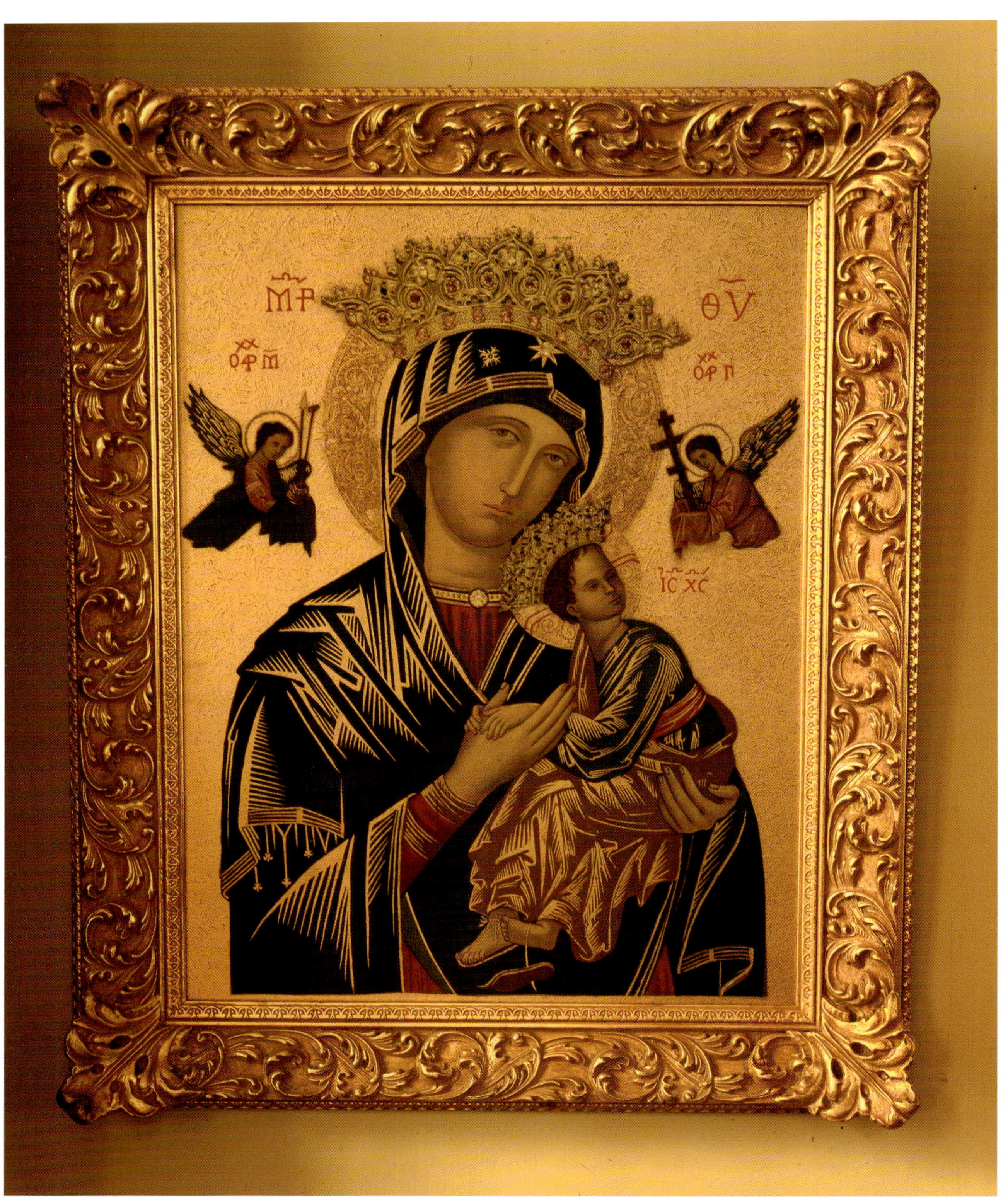

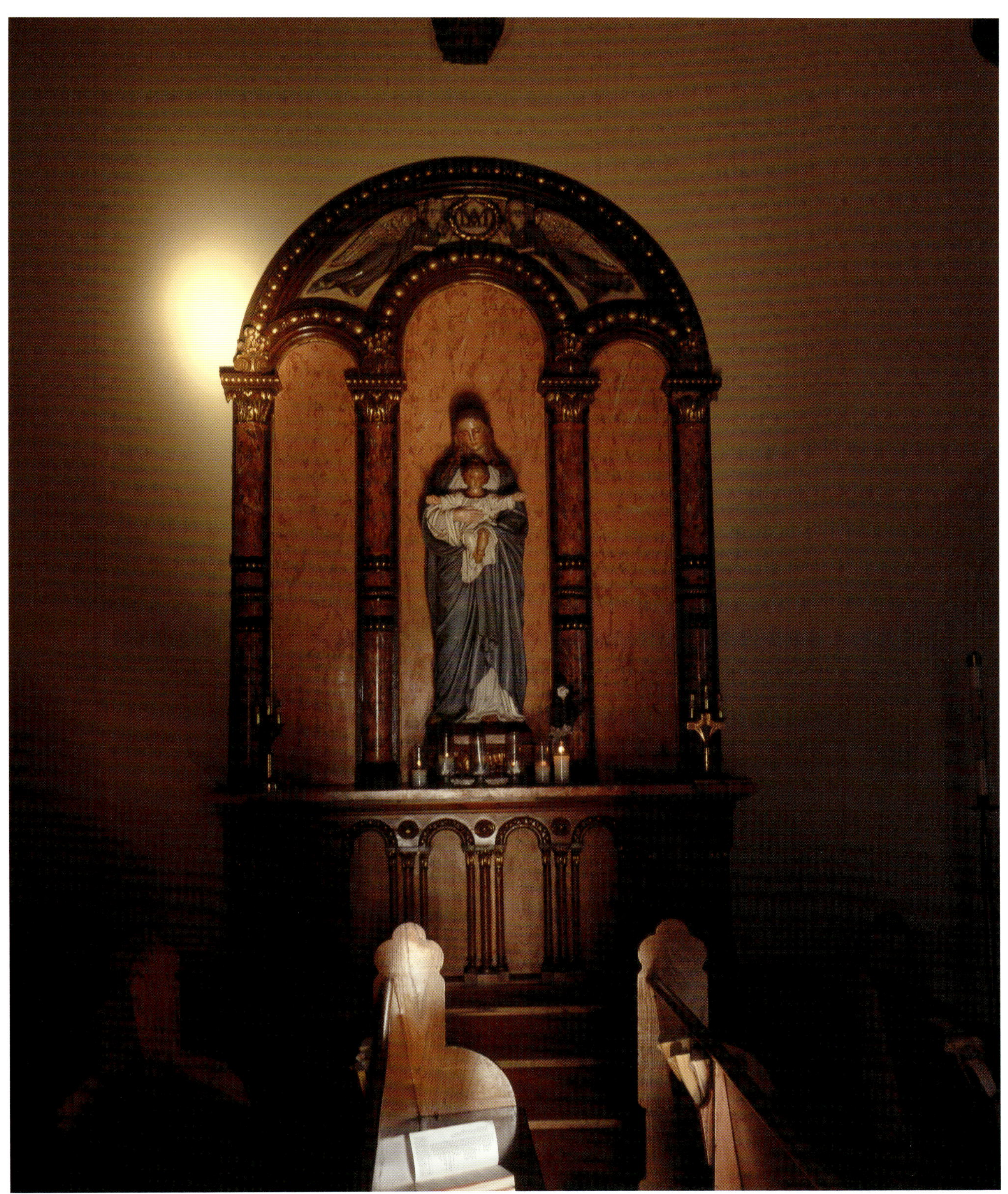

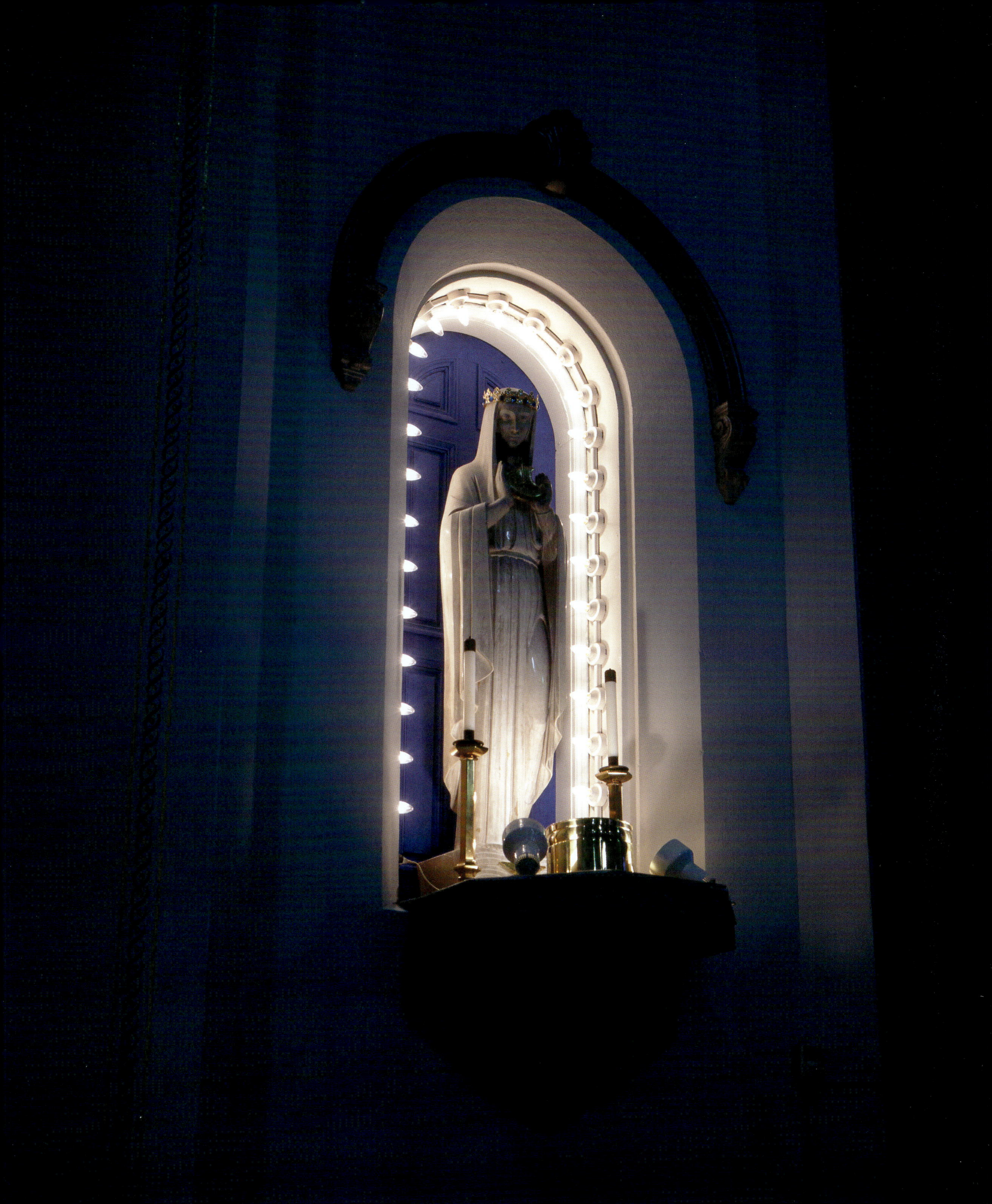

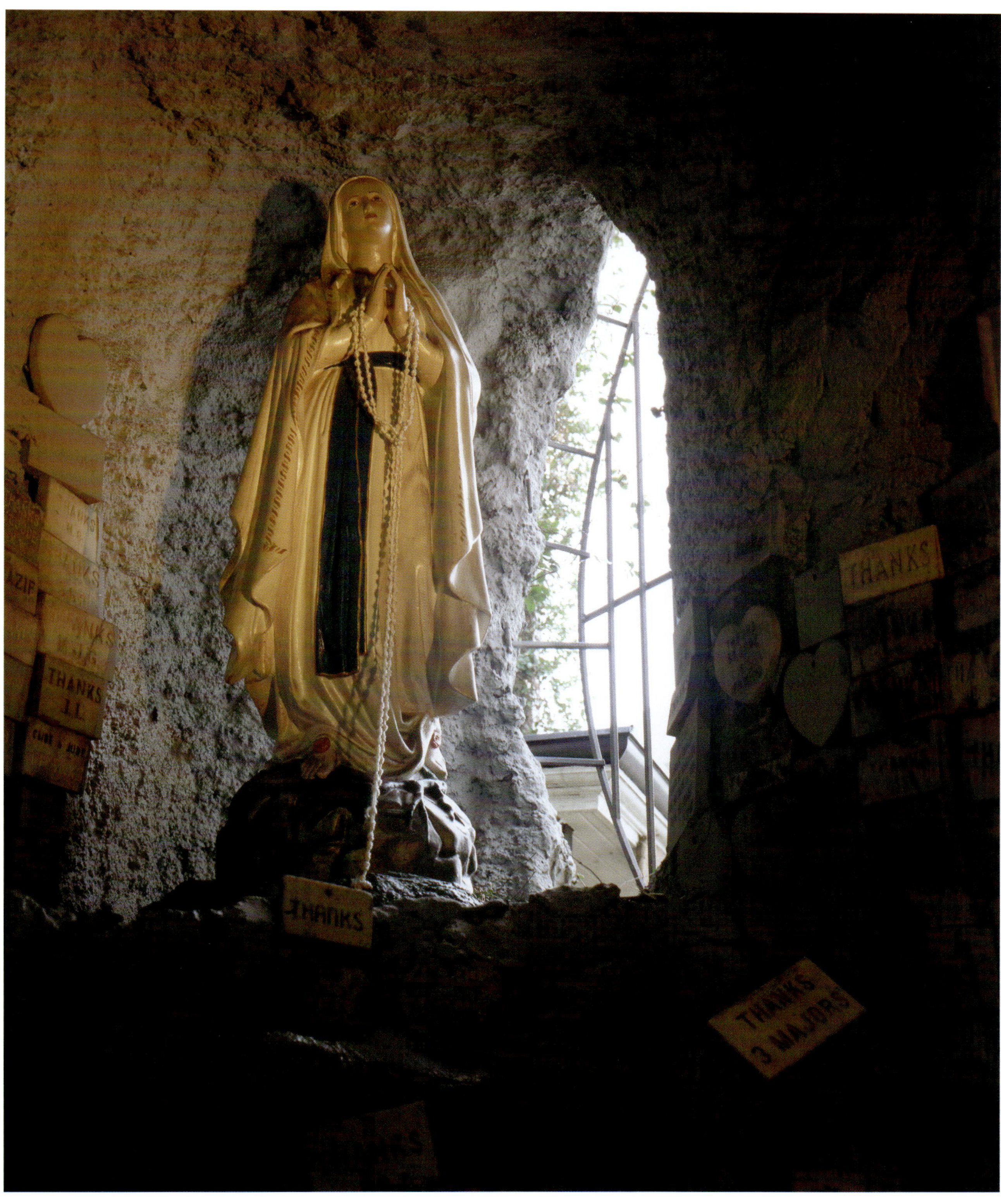
THANKS
THANKS
I.L.
THANKS
THANKS
3 MAJORS

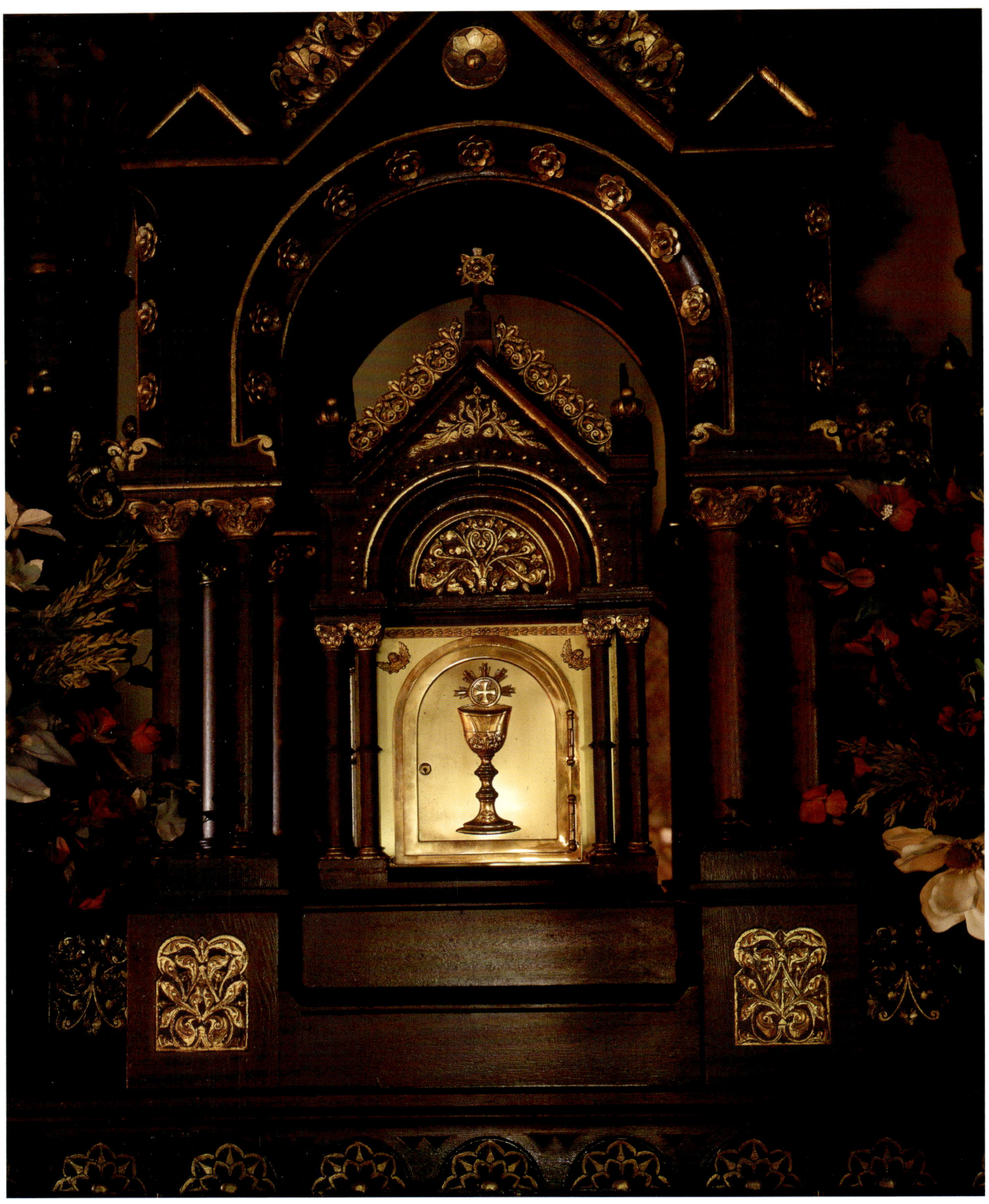

Light

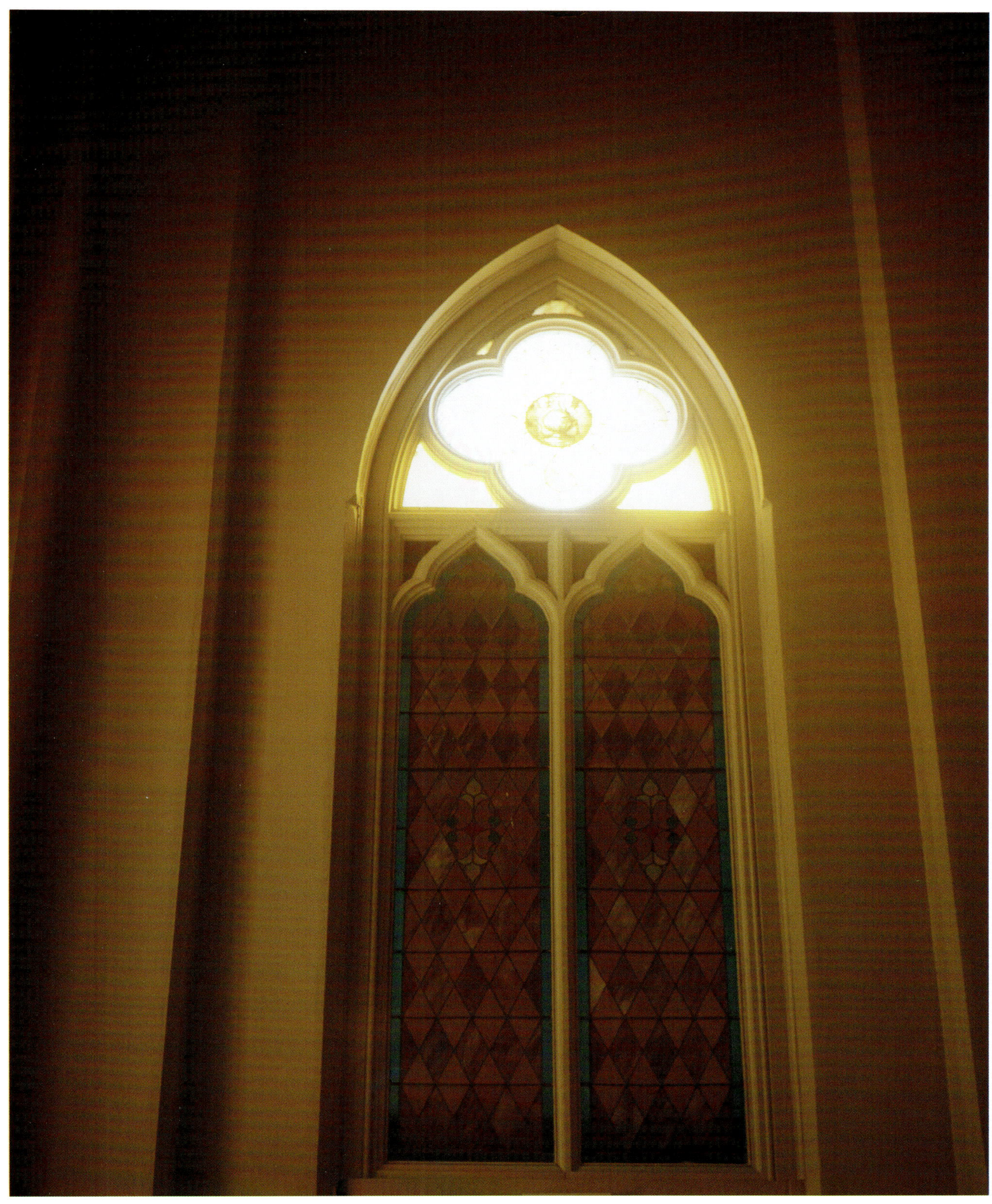

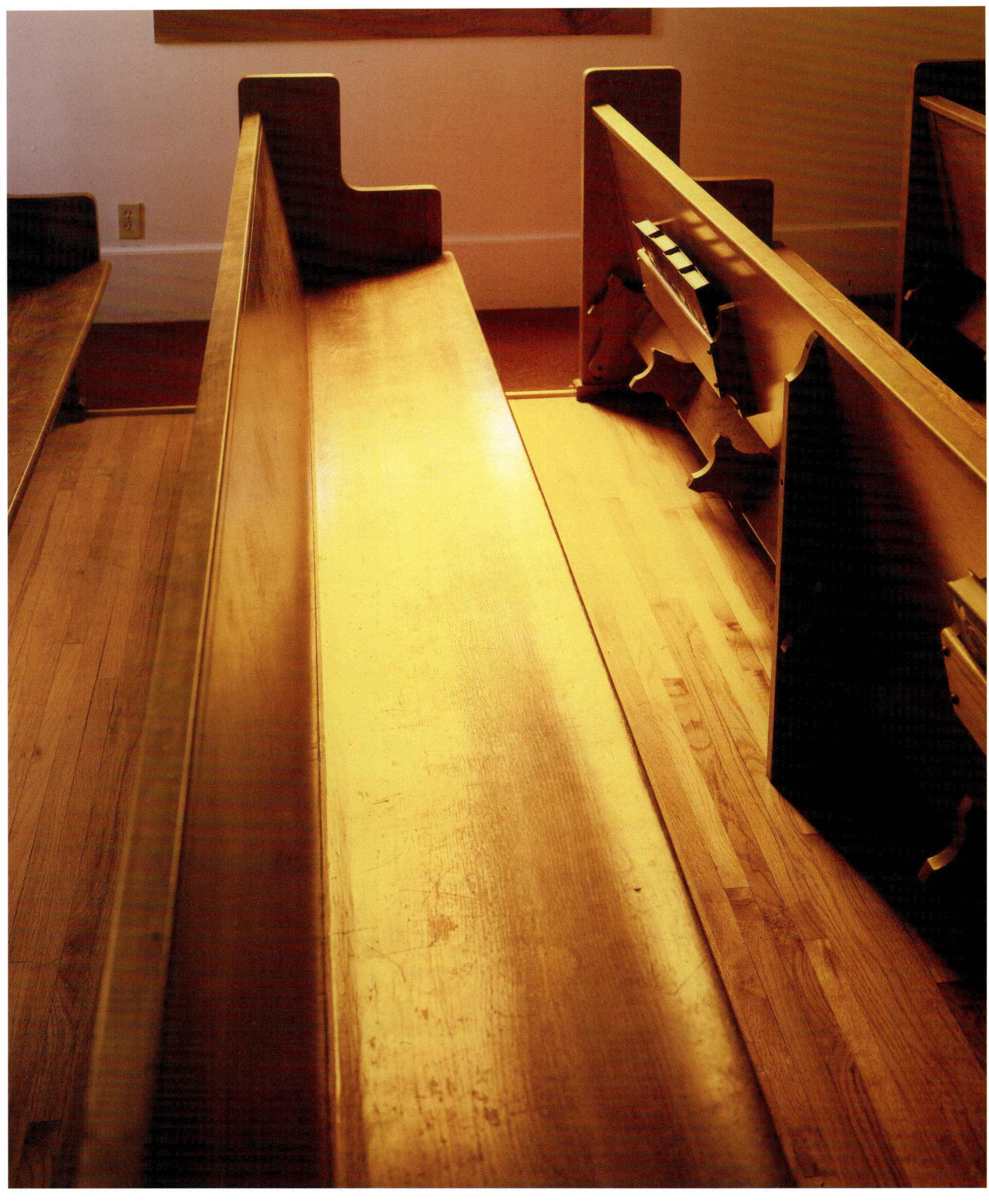

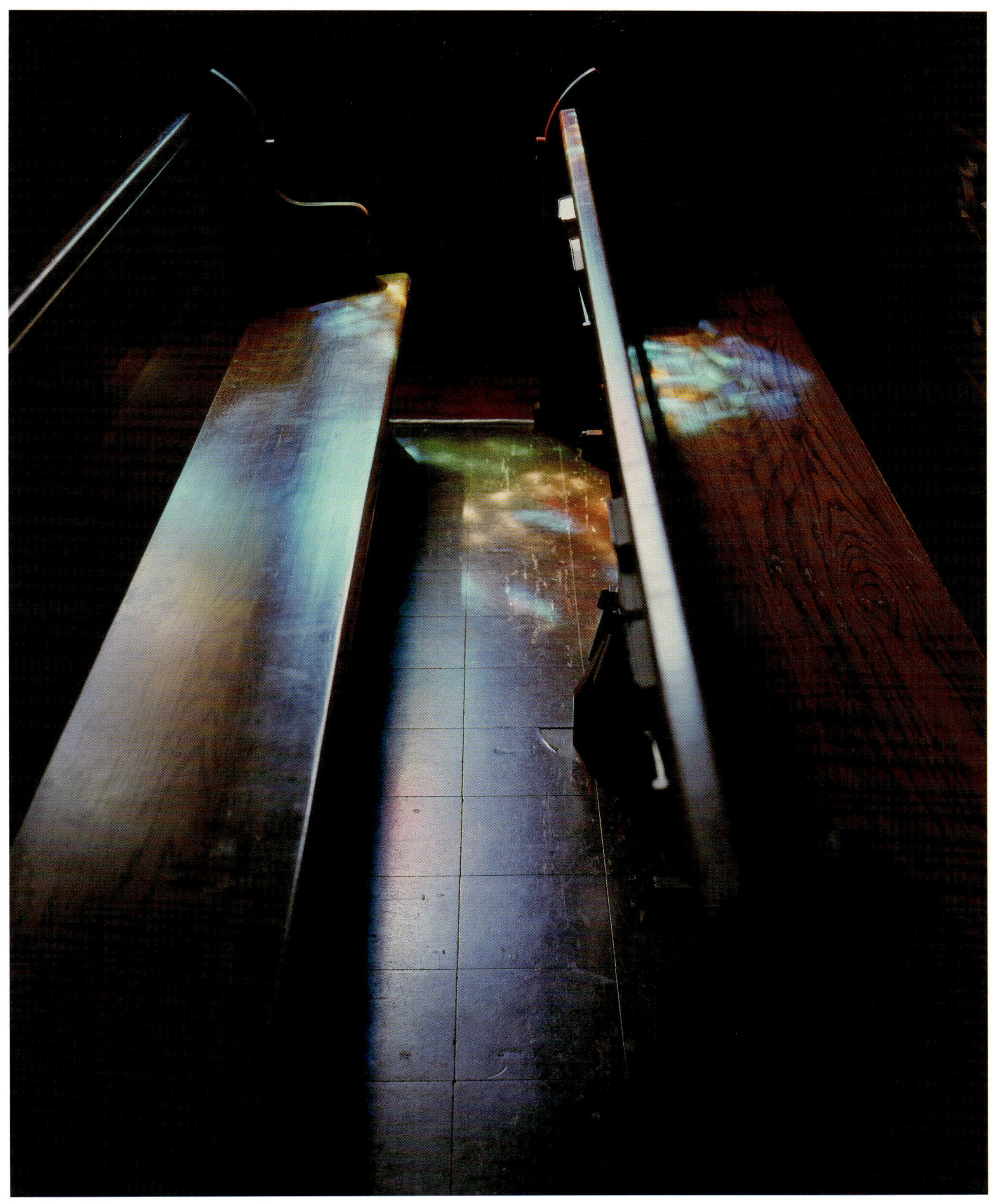

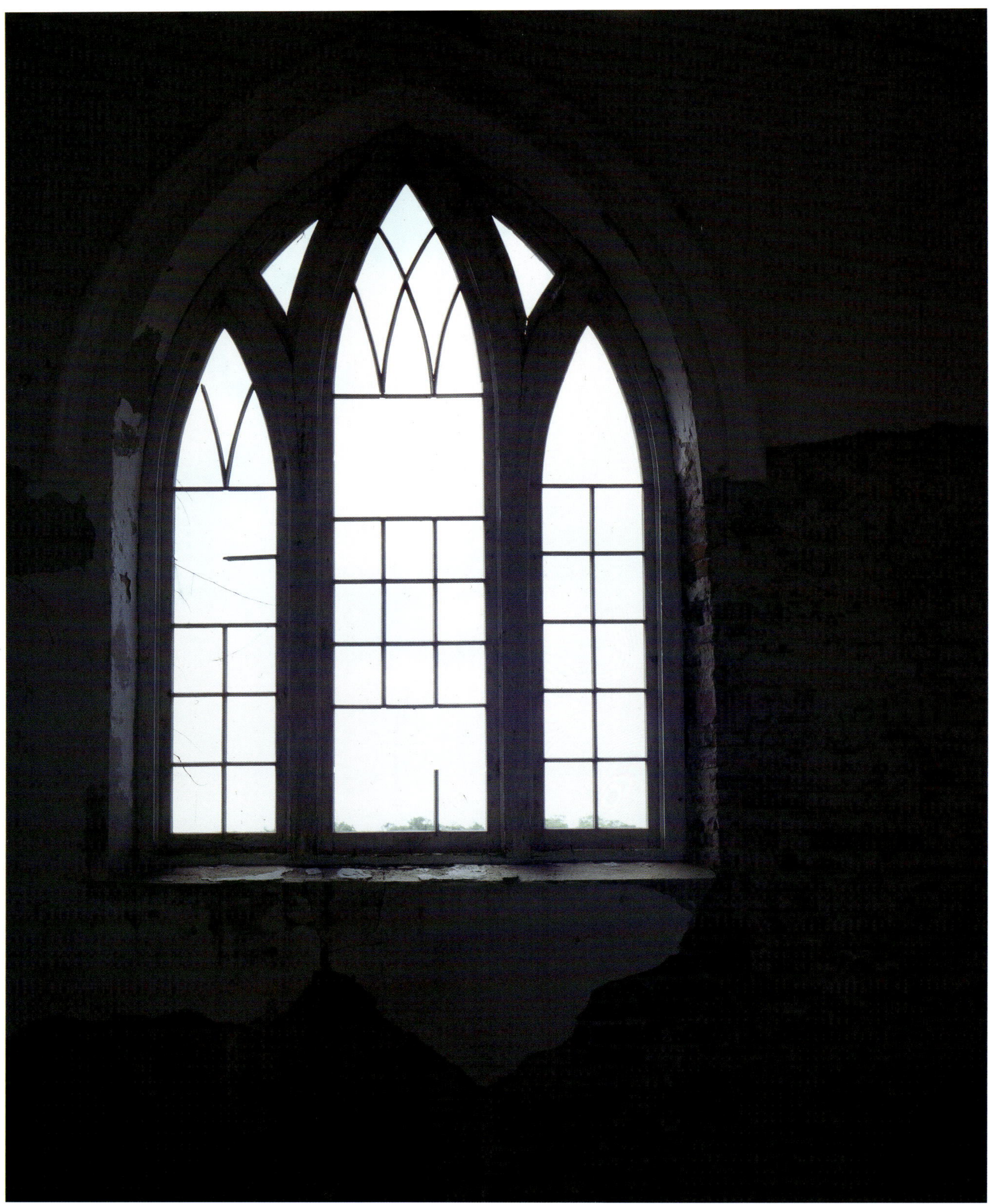

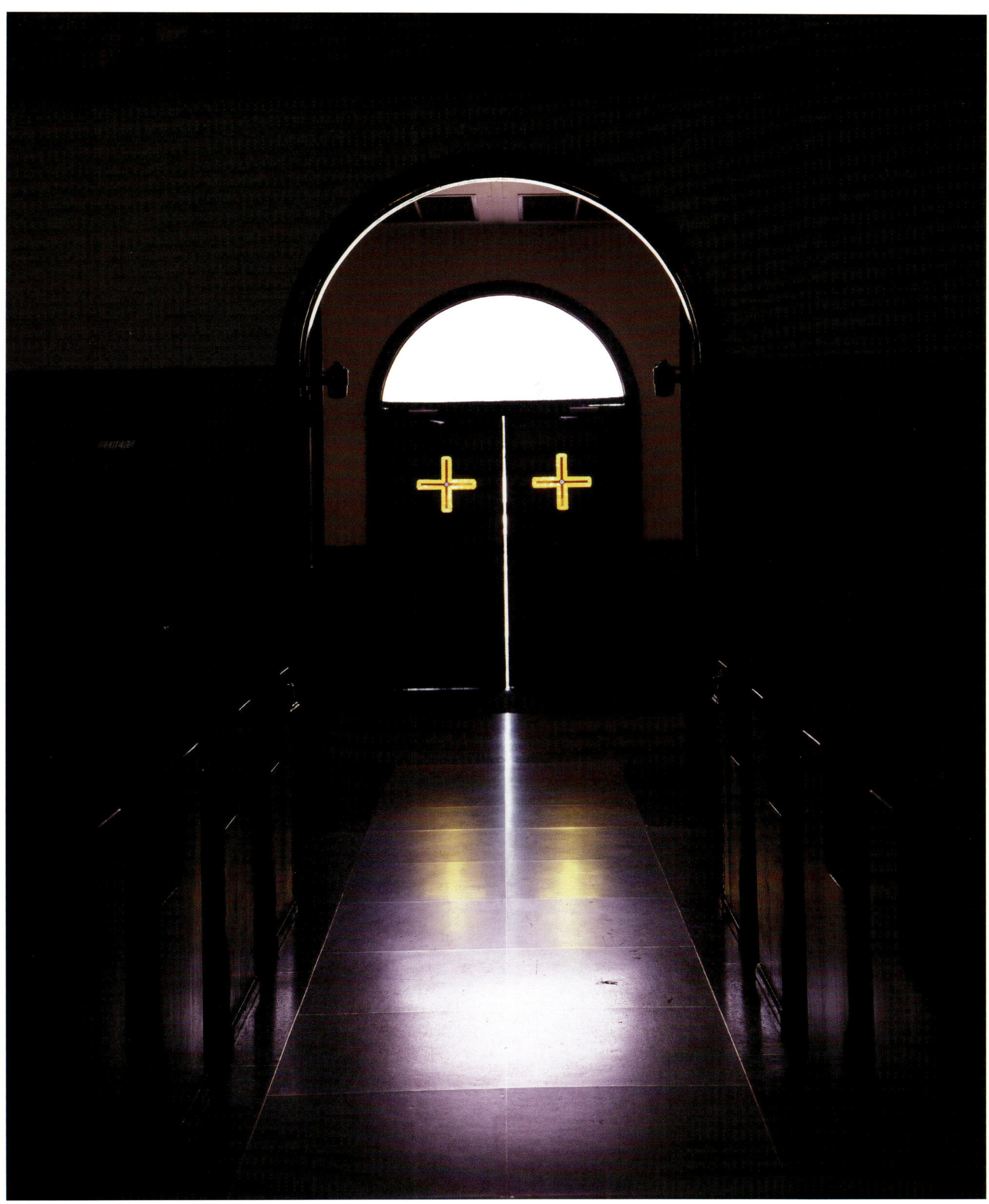

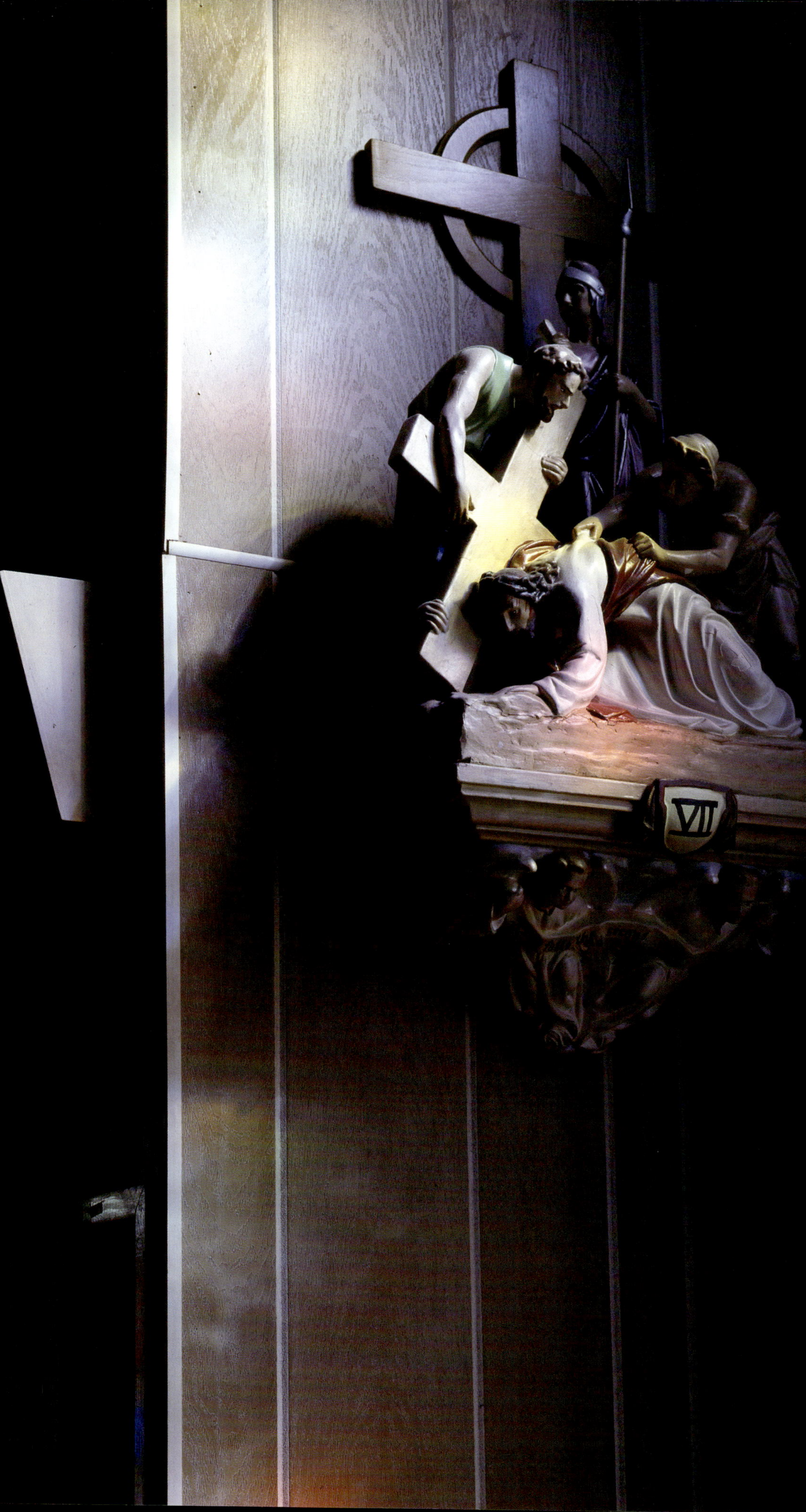

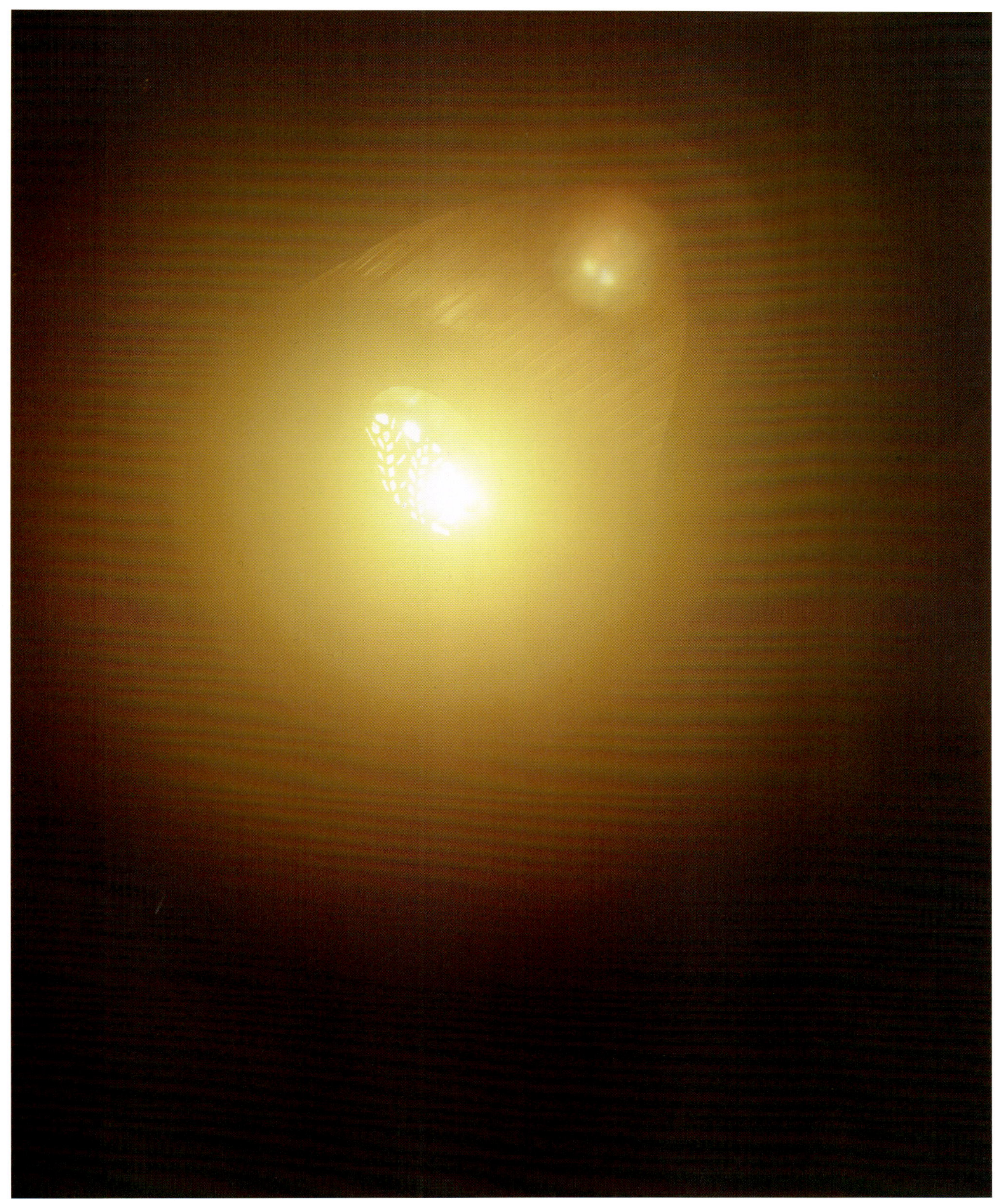

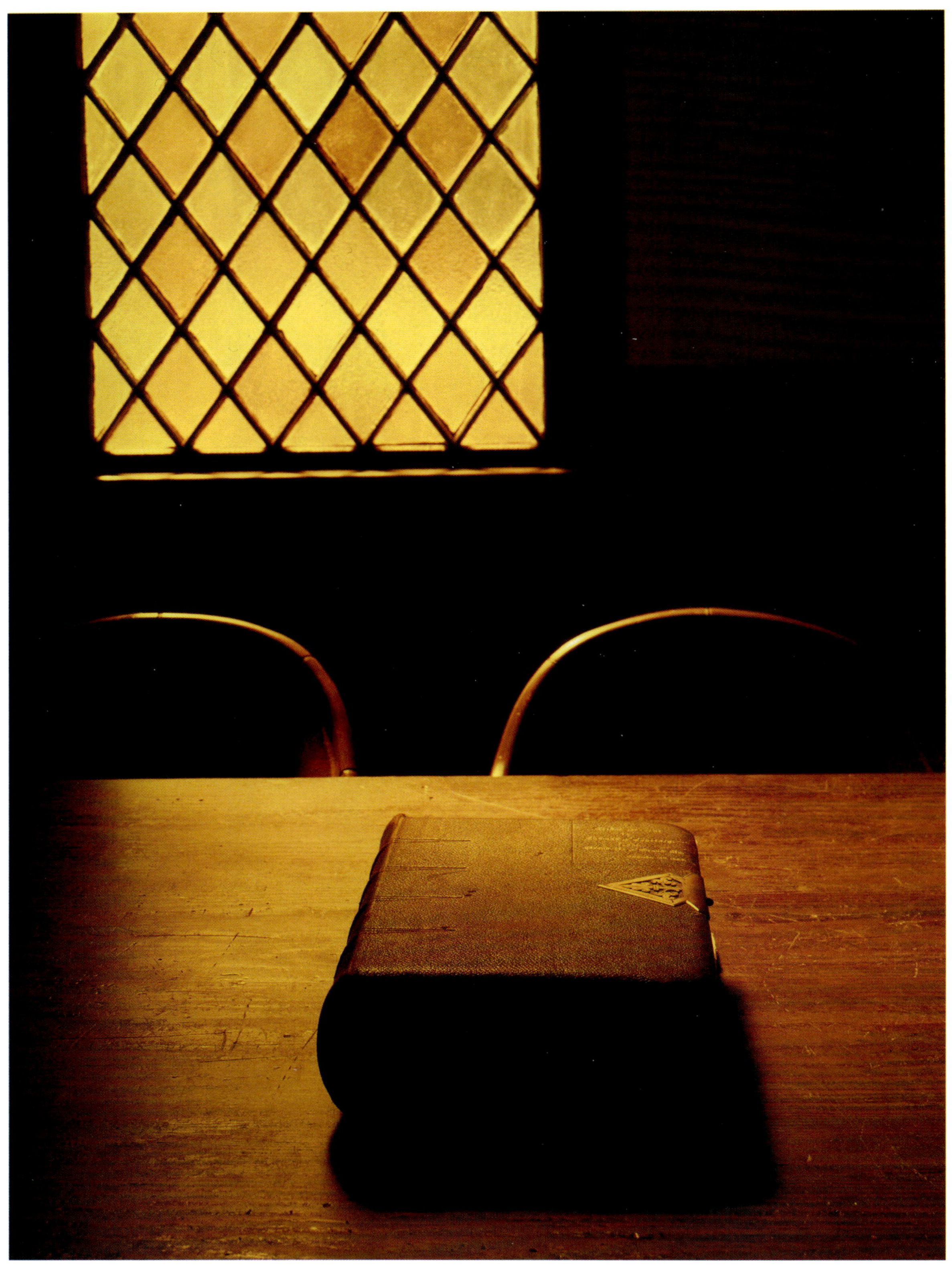

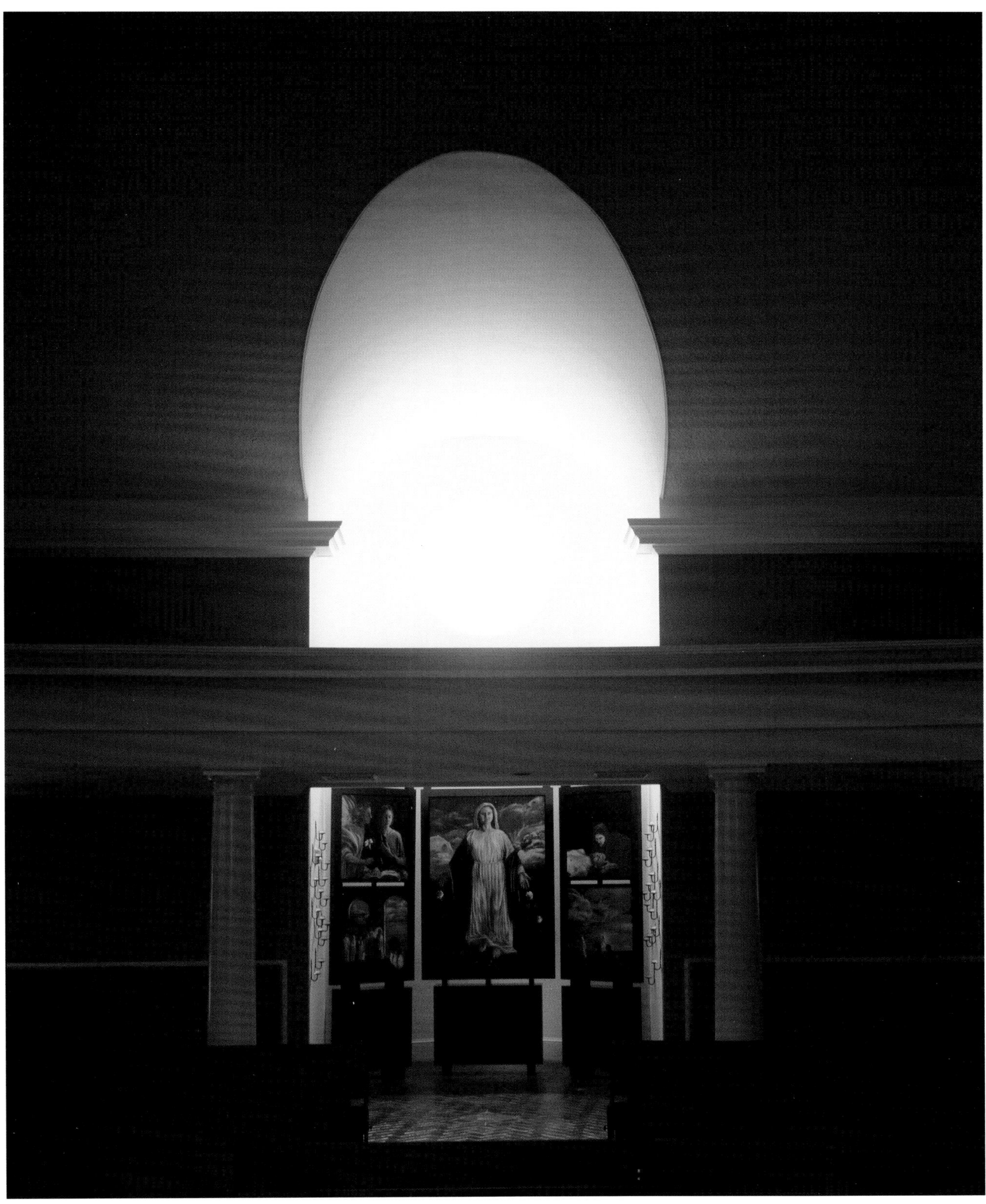

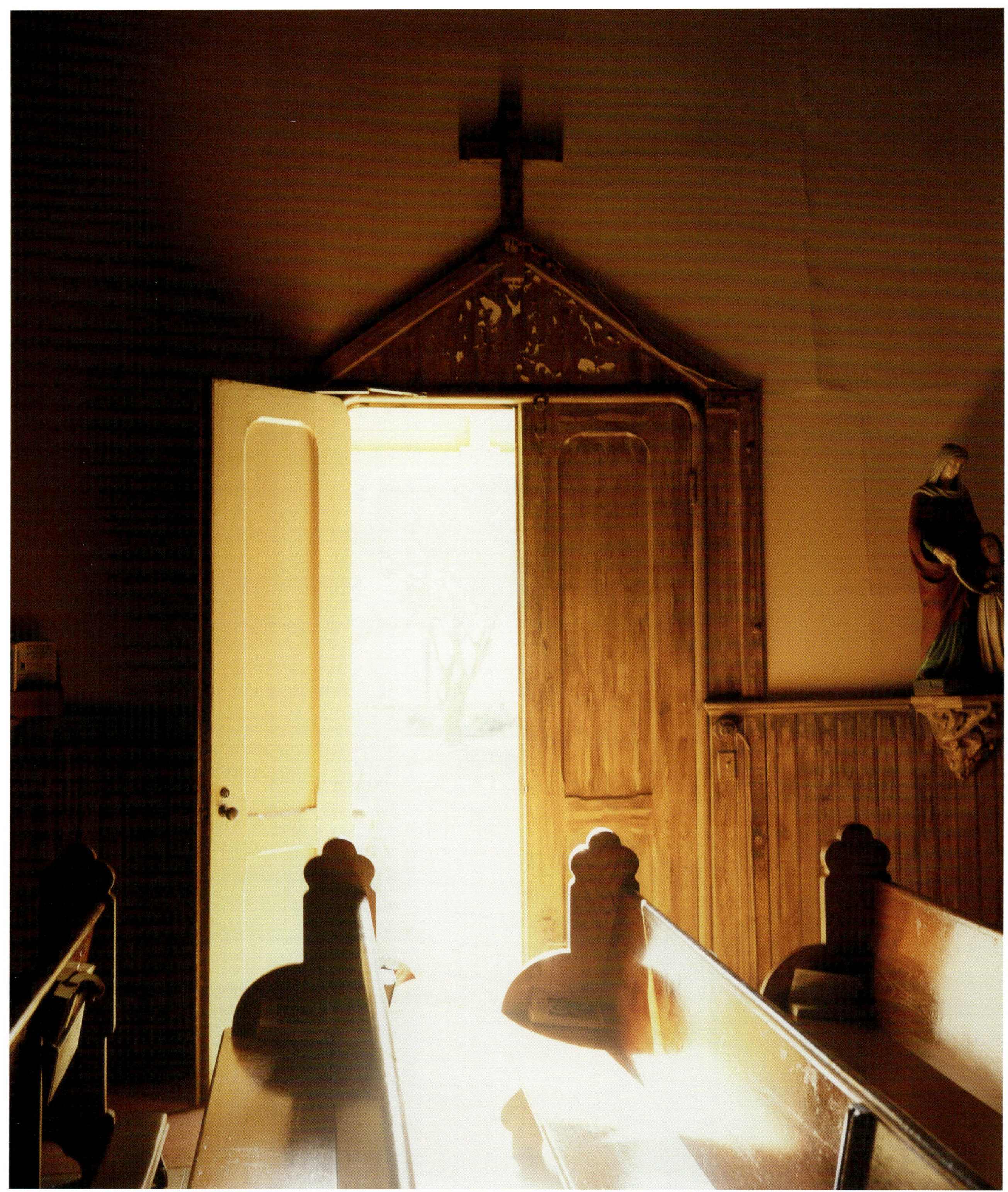

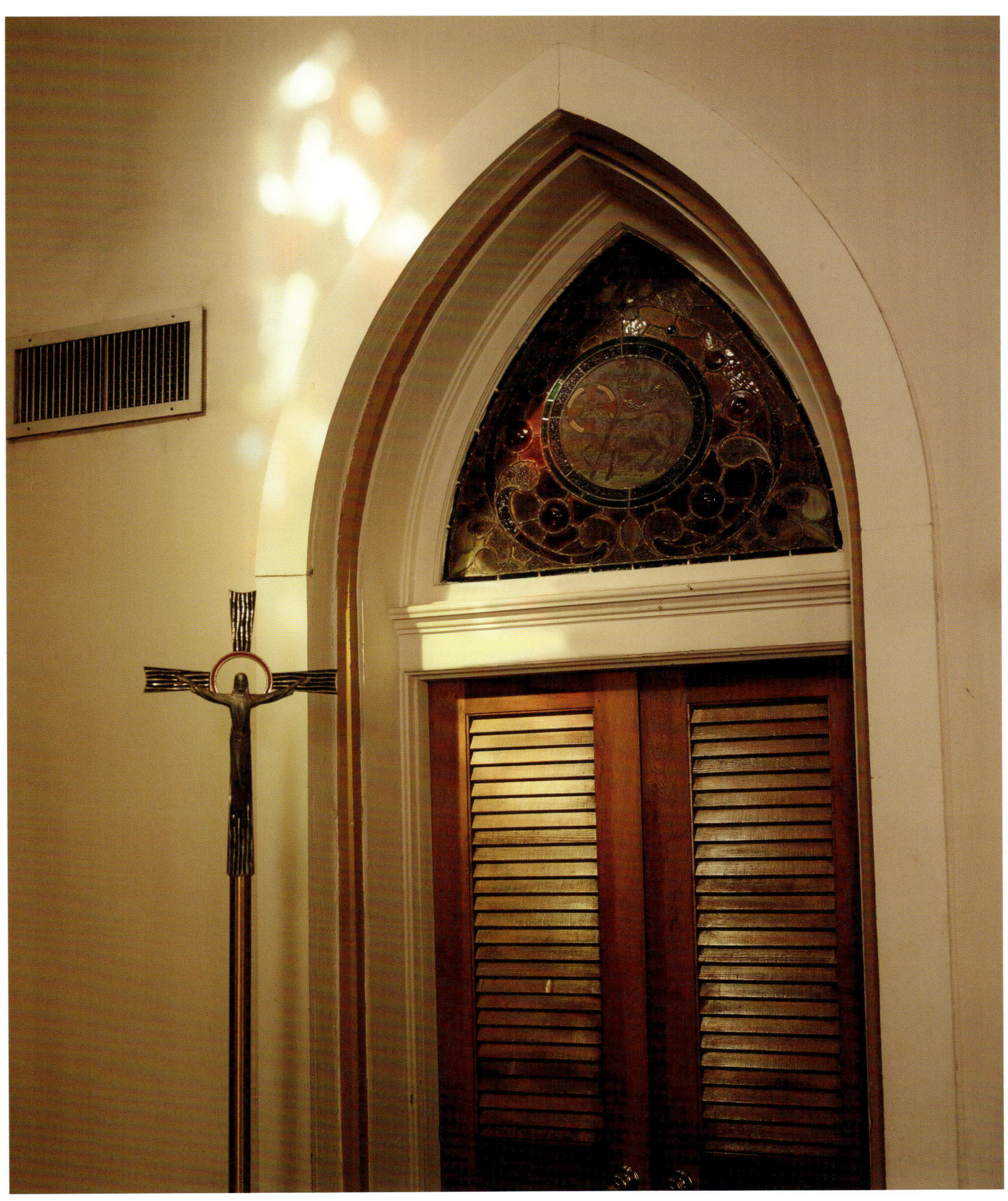

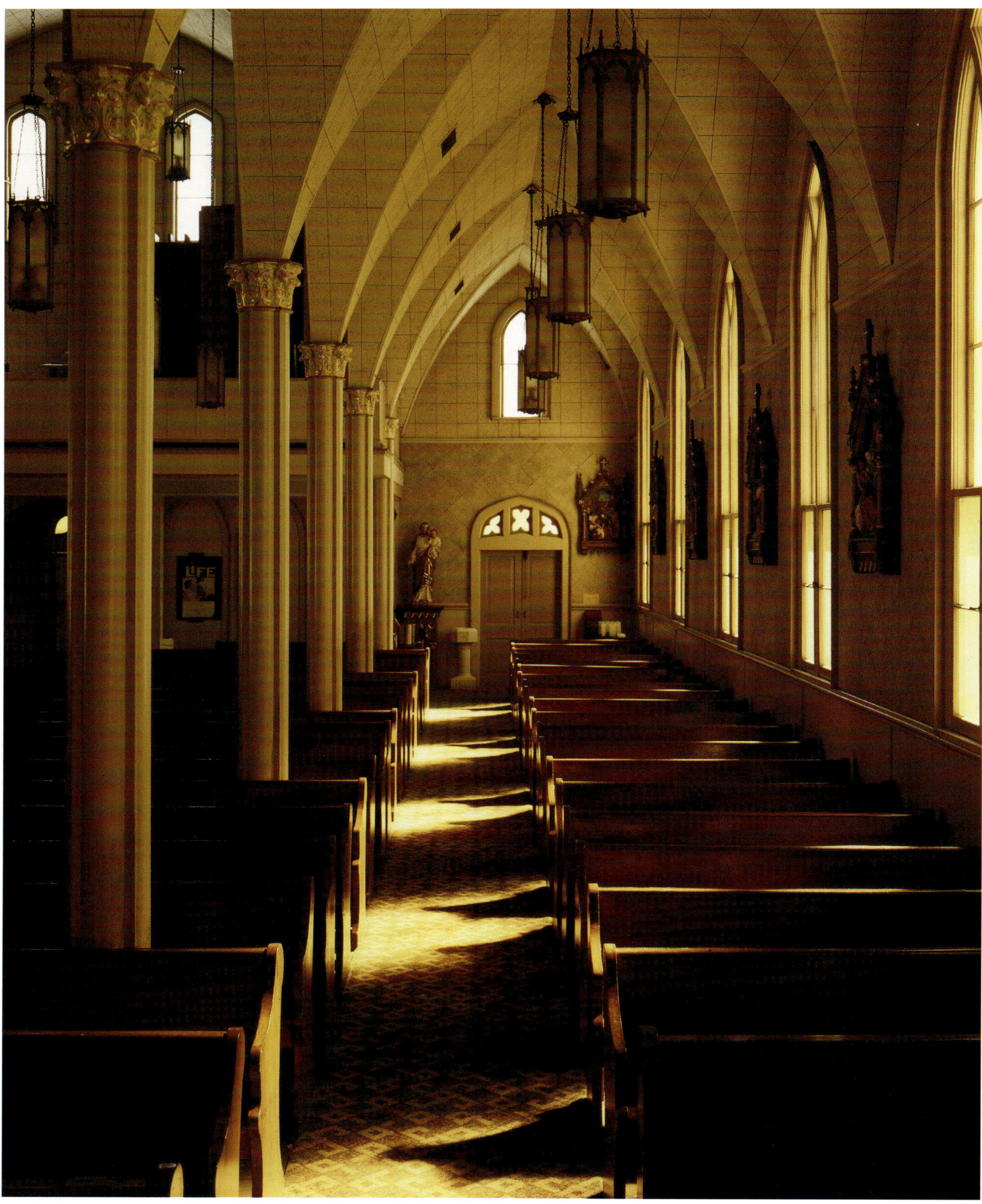

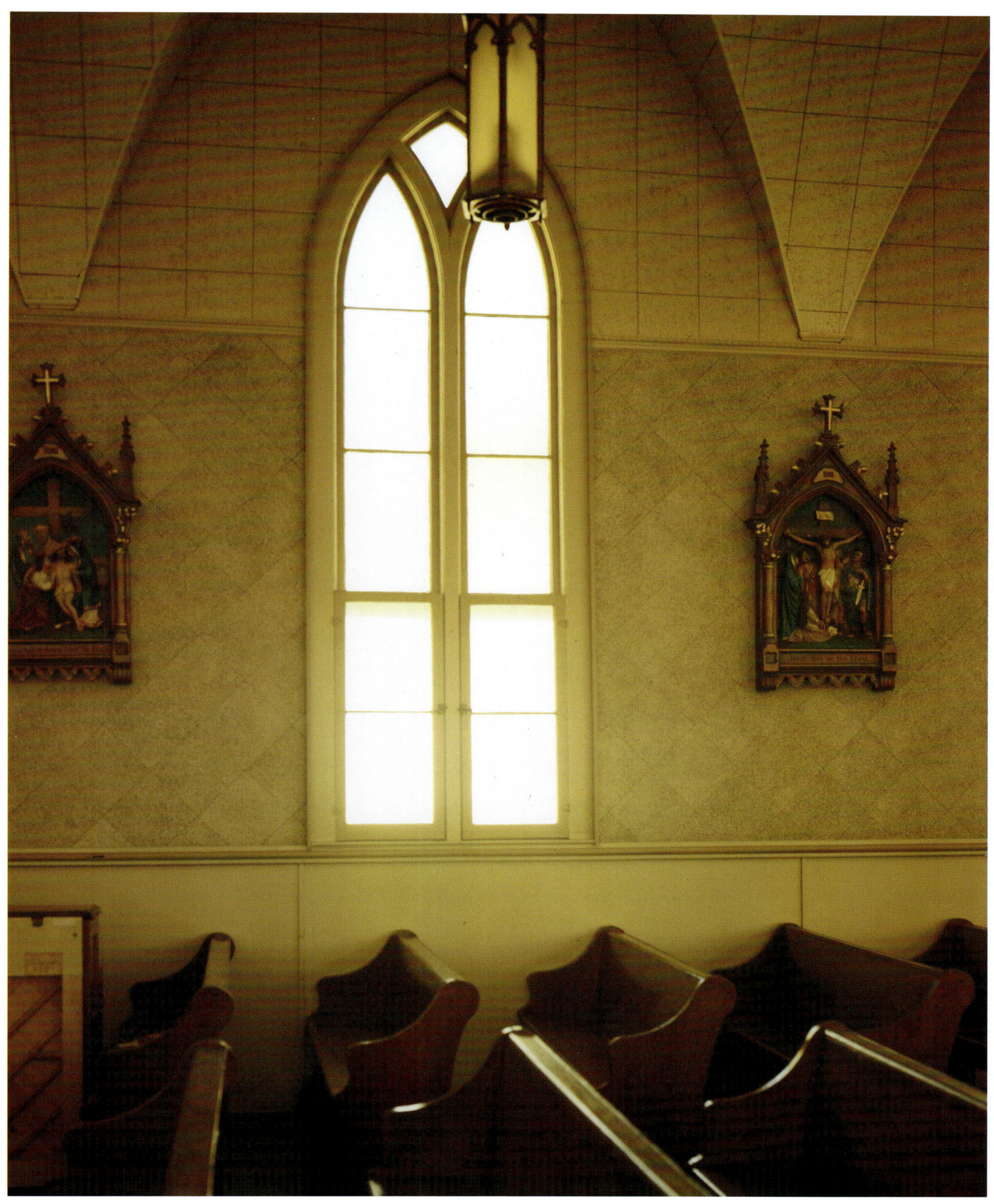

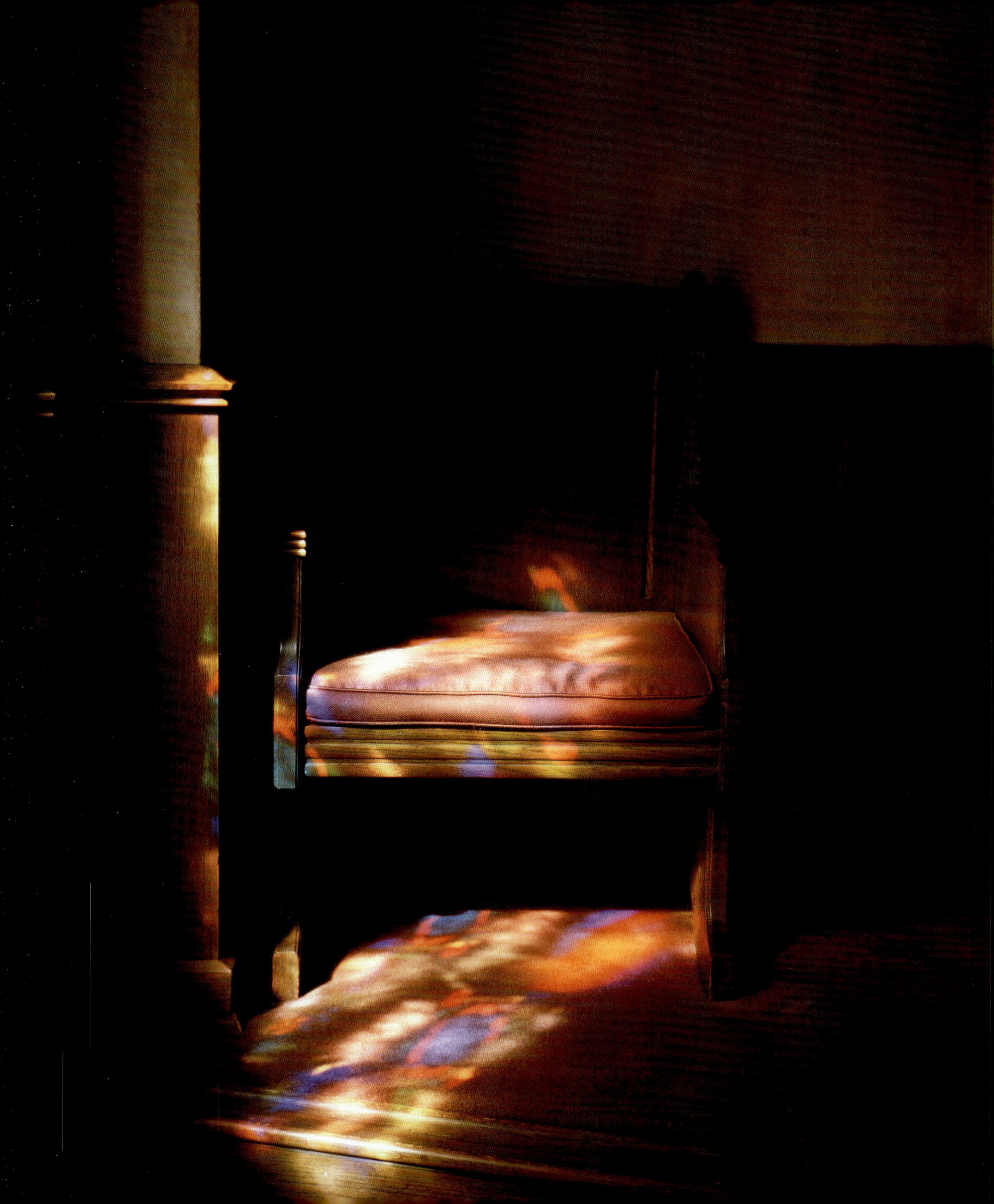

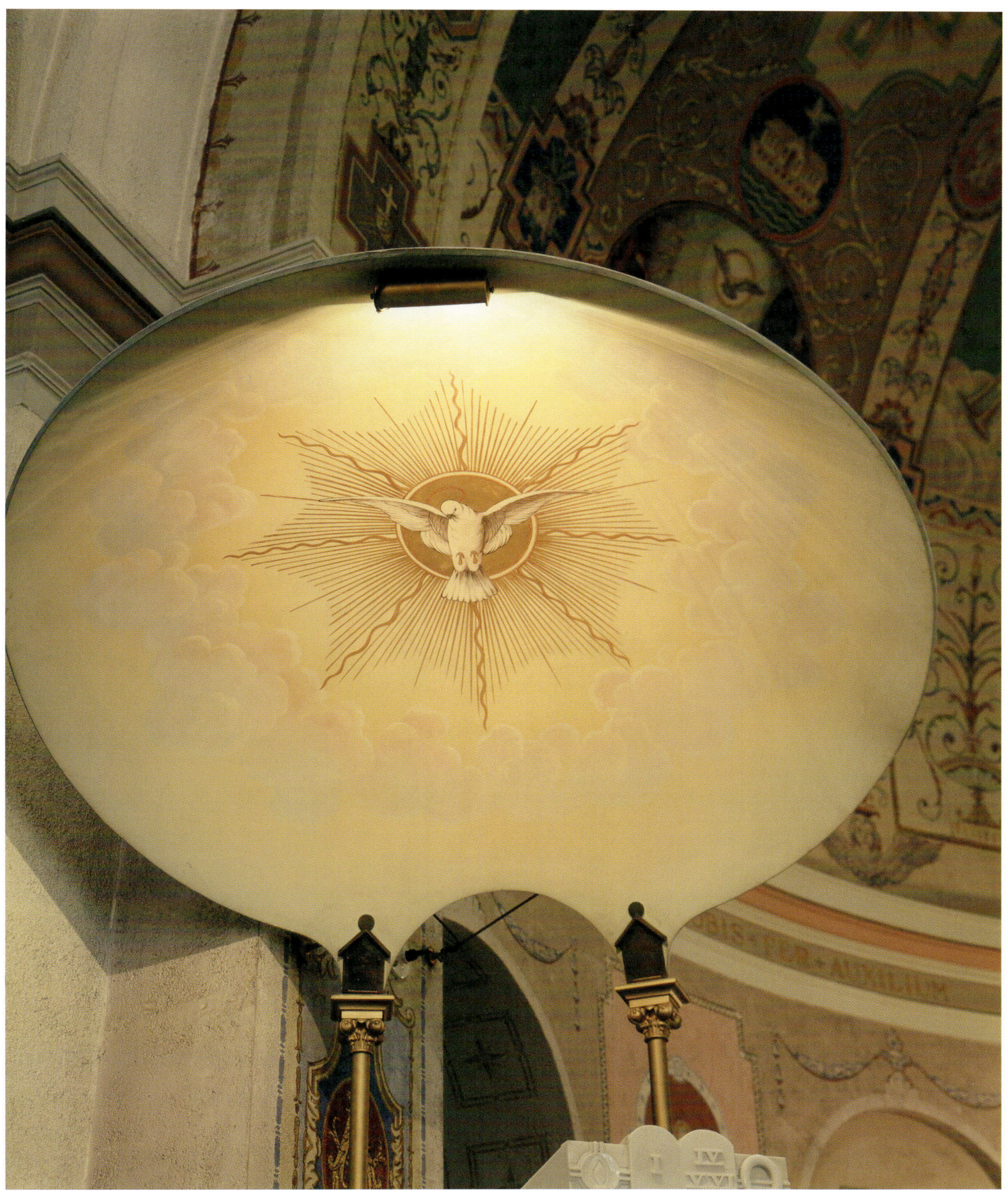

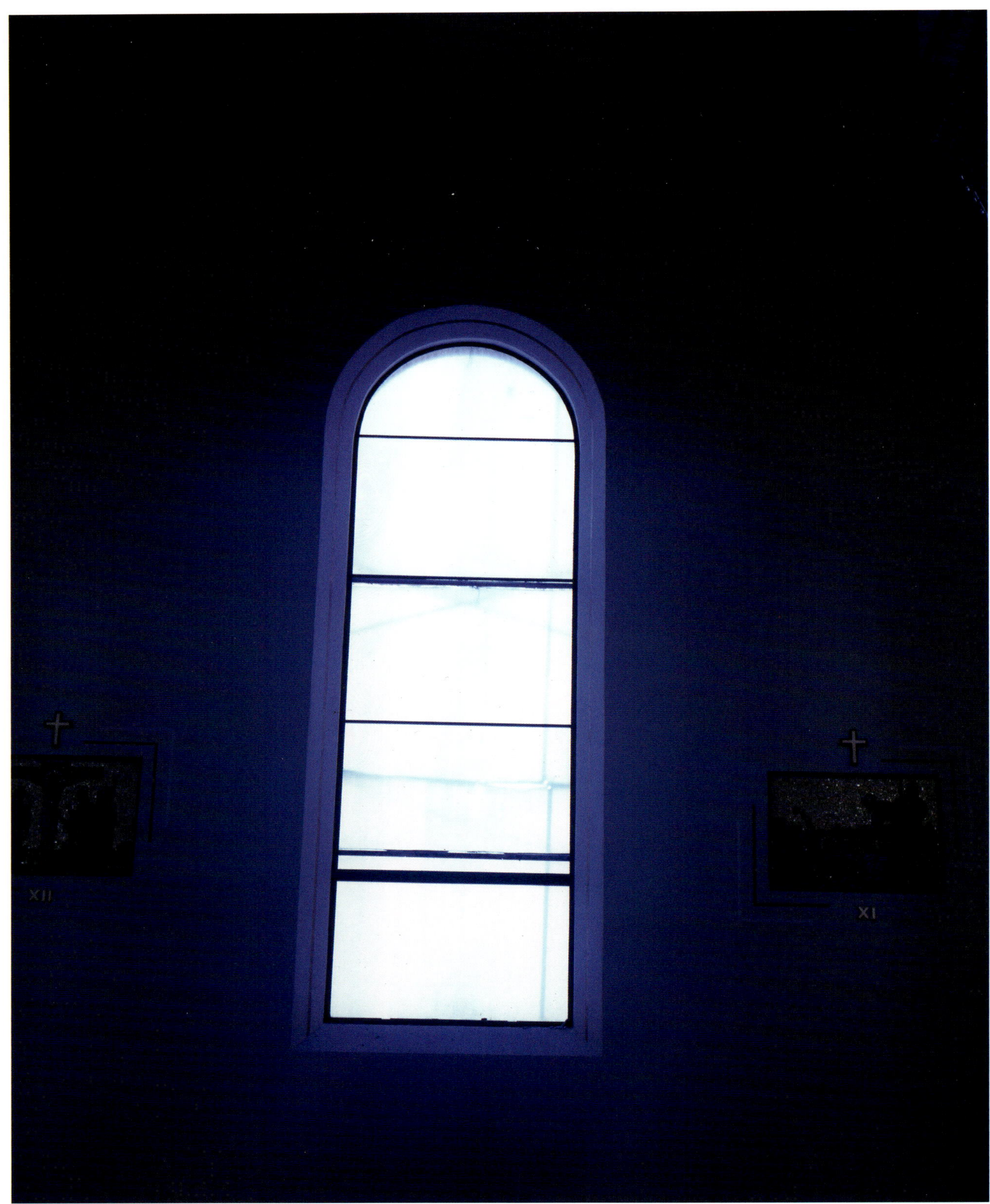

XII
XI

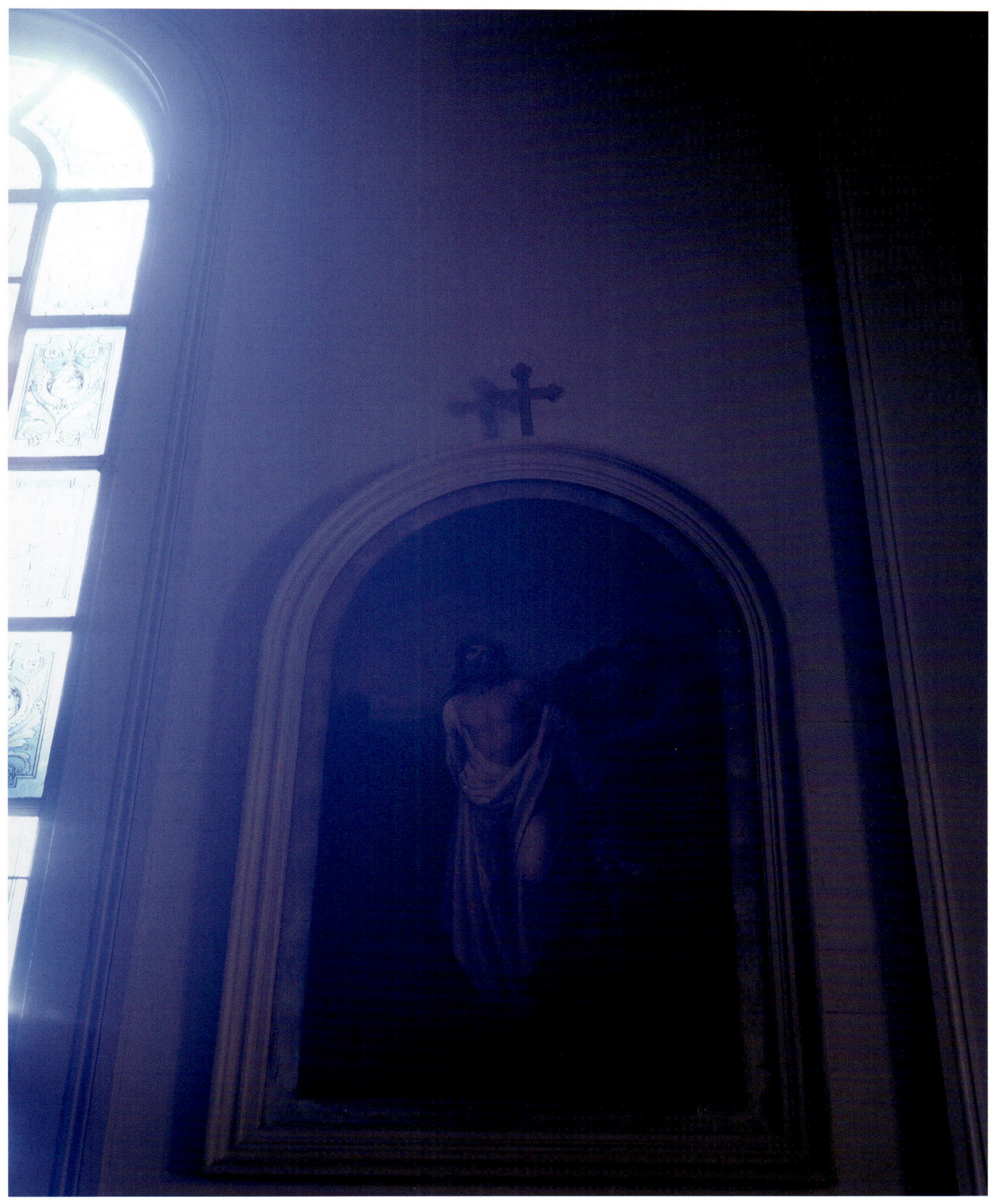

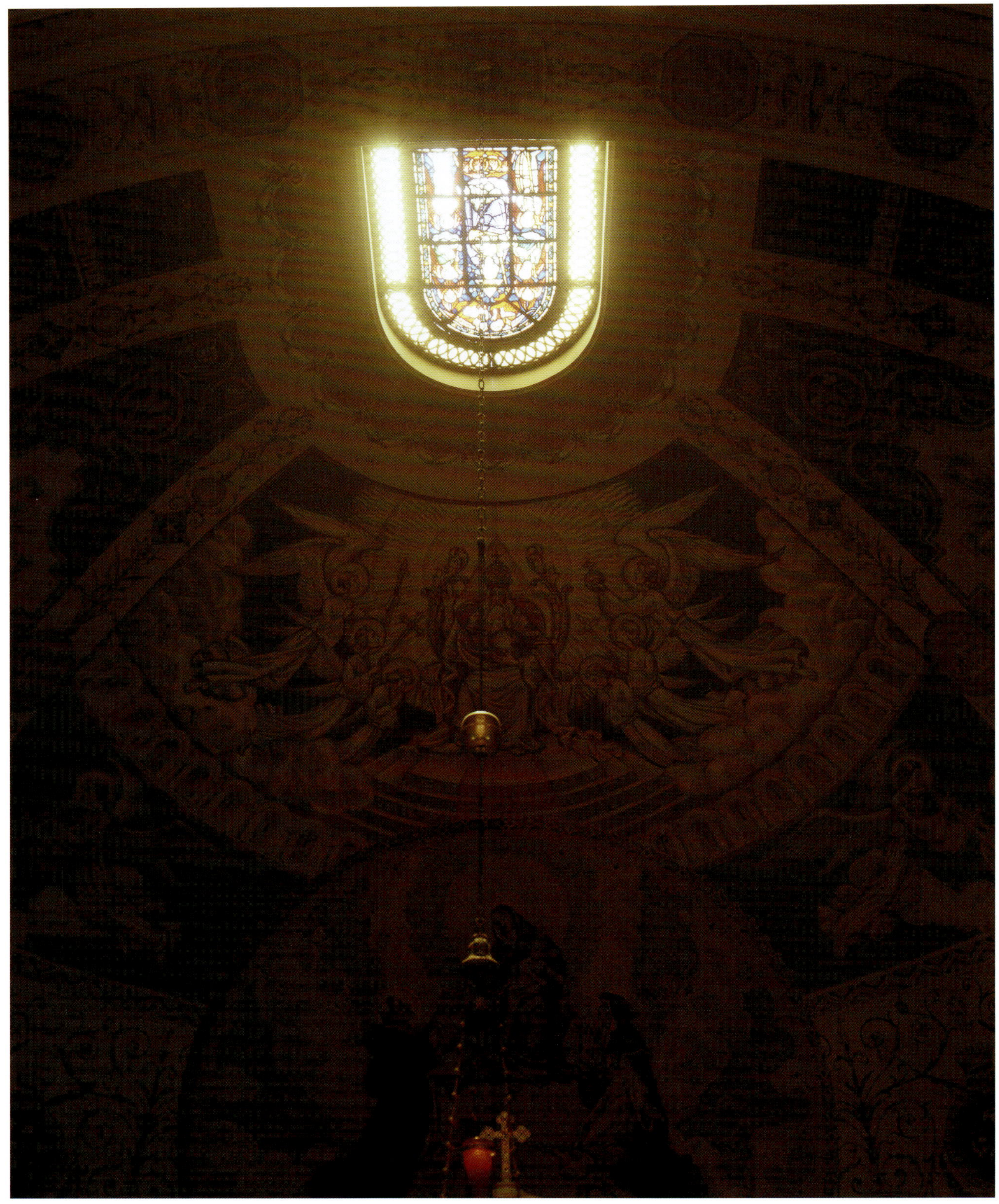

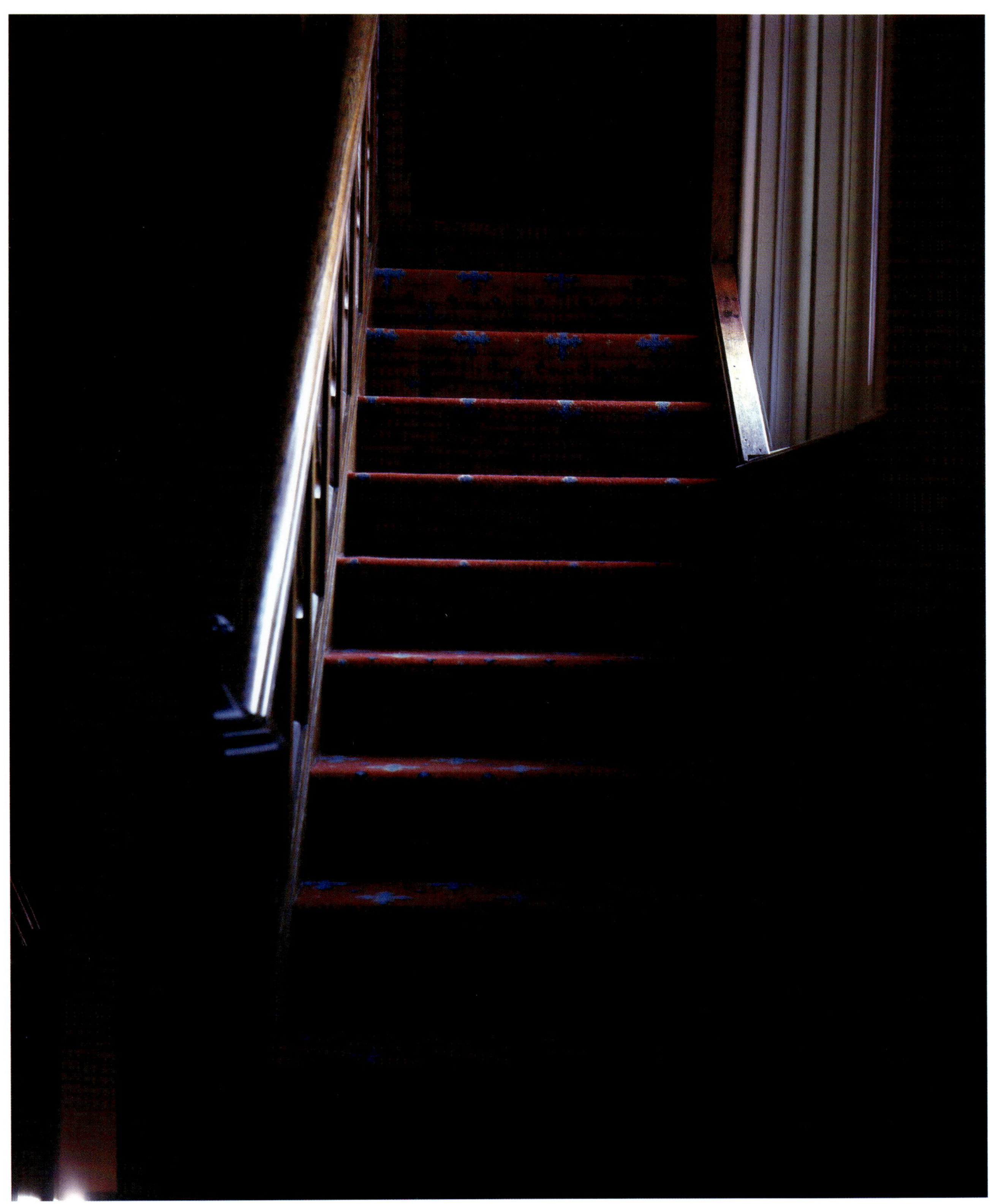

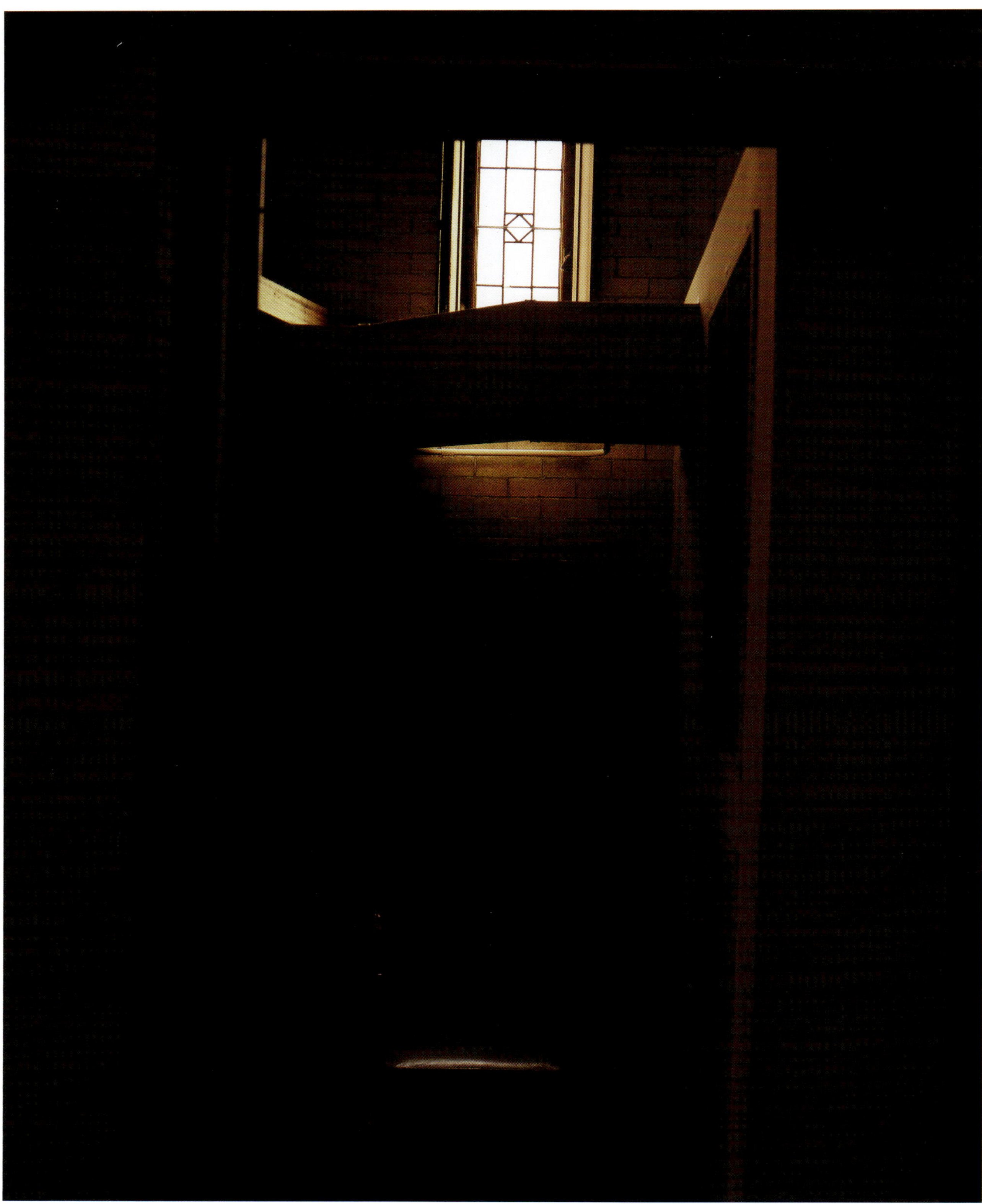

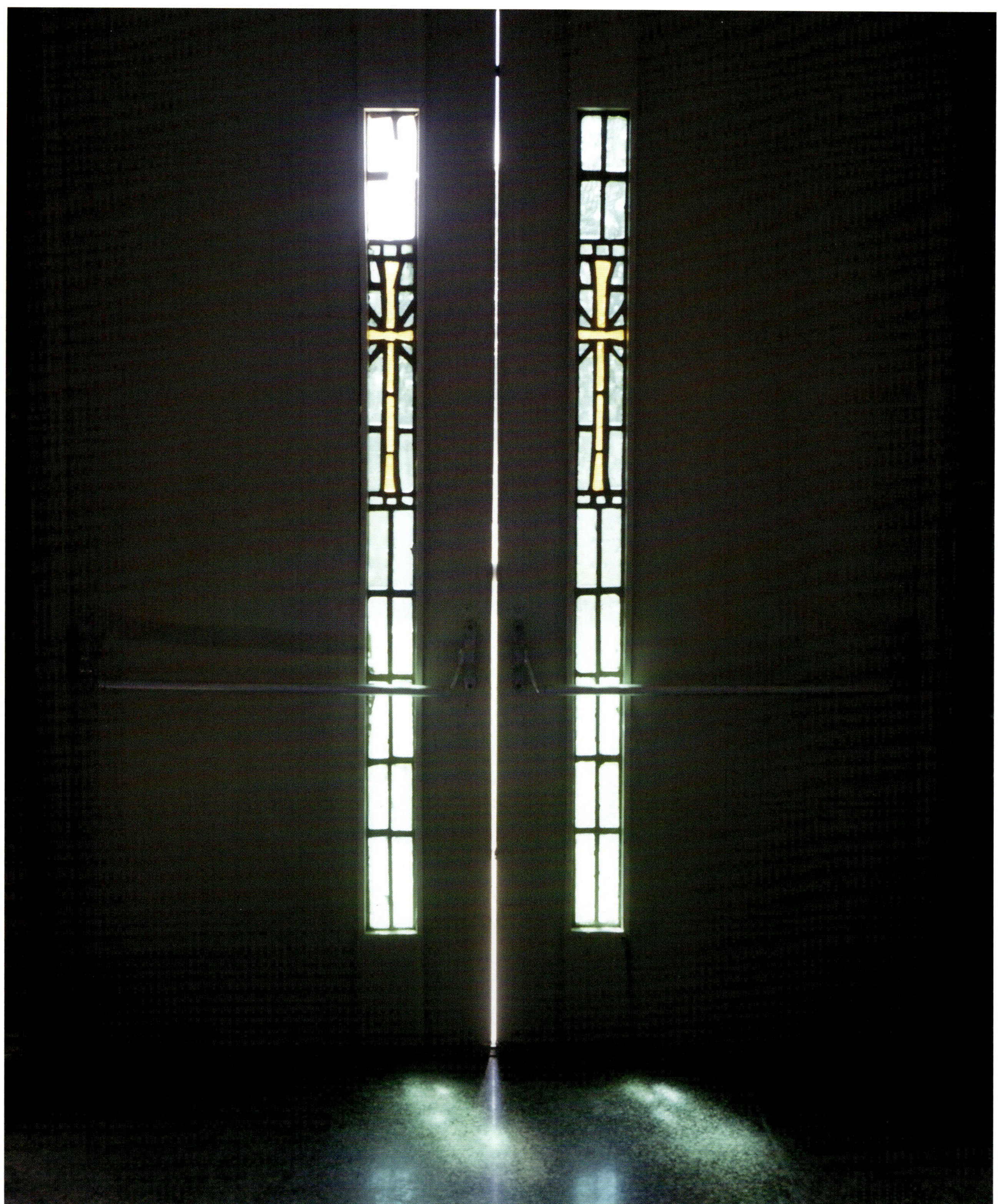

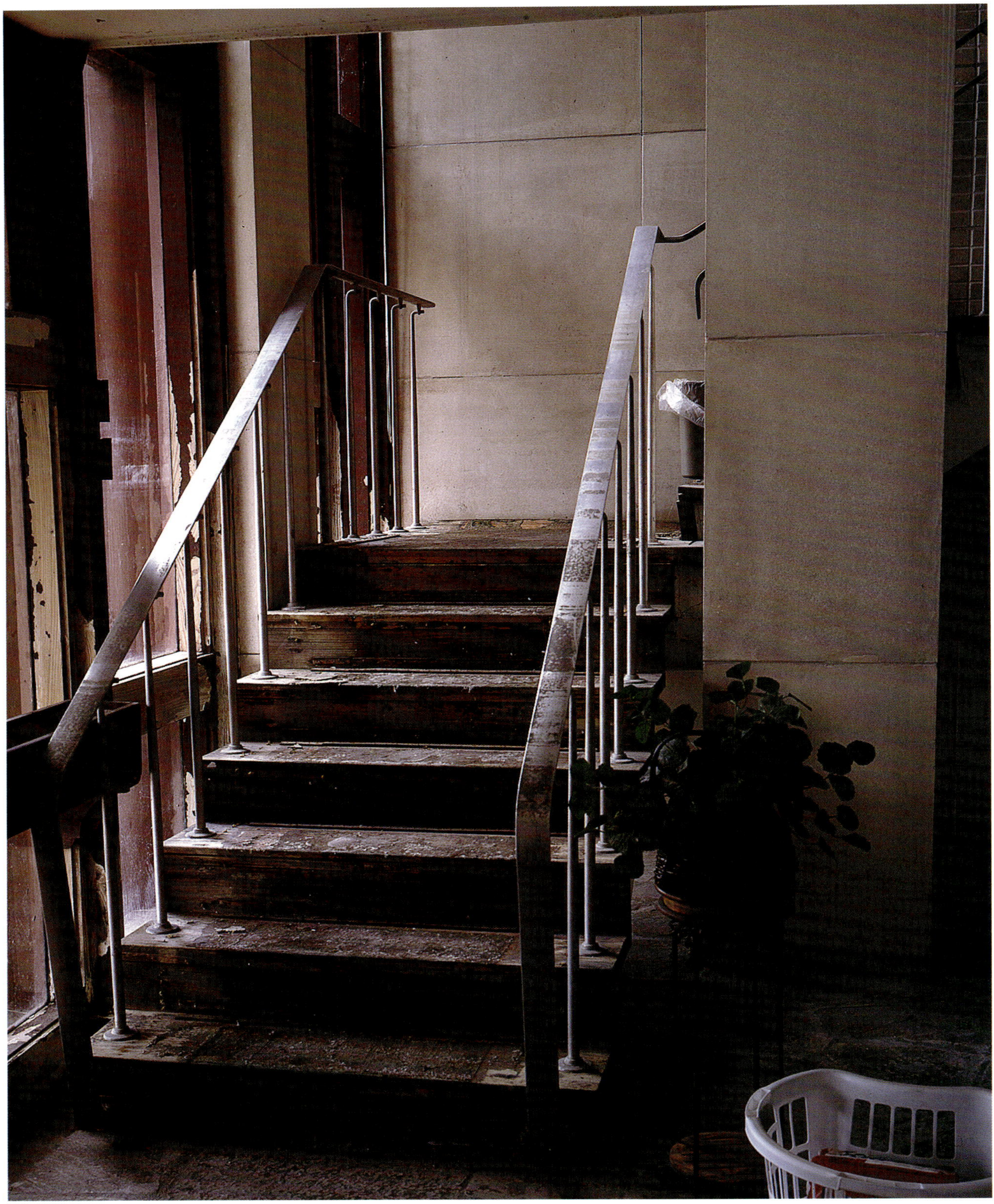

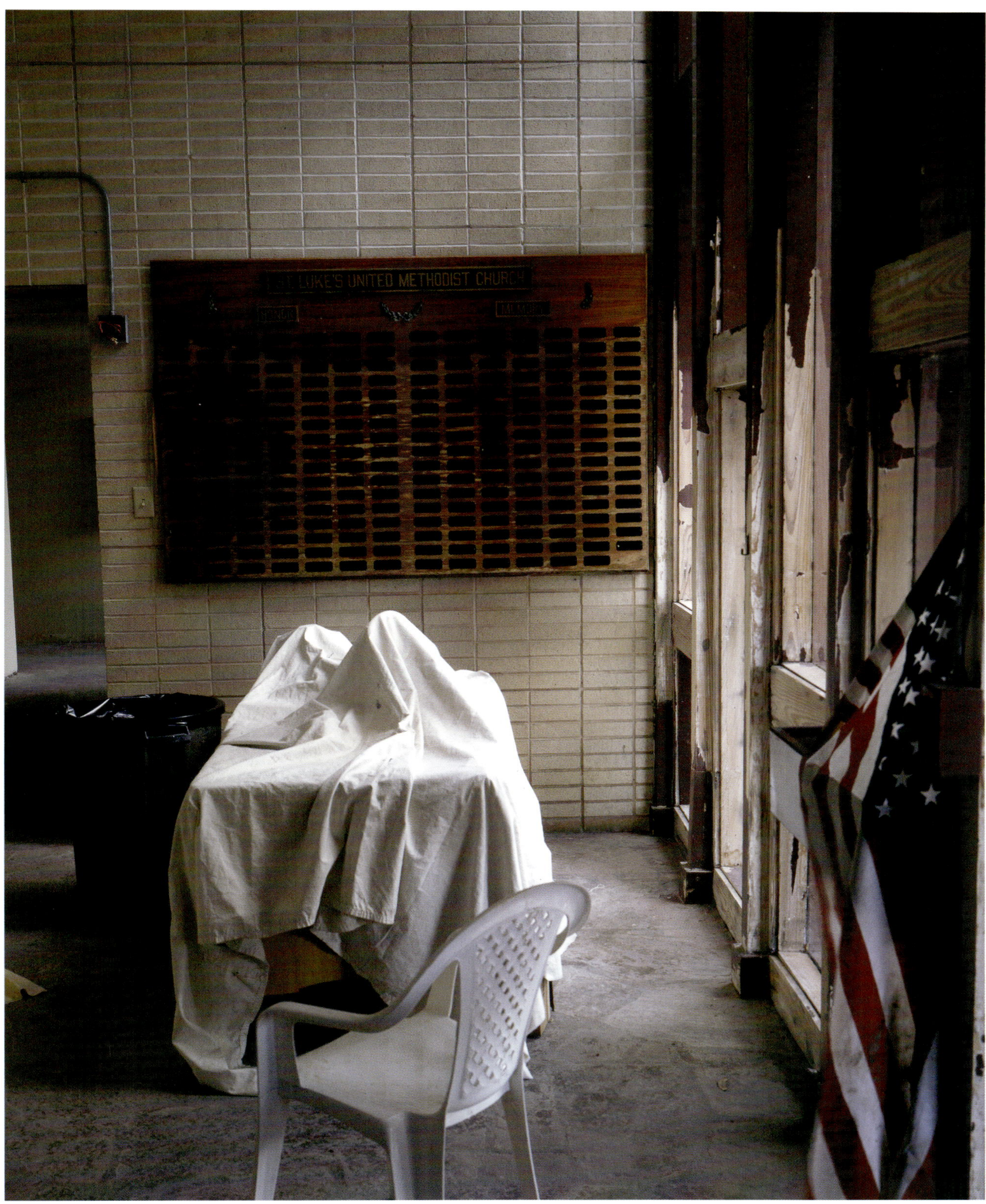
ST. LUKE'S UNITED METHODIST CHURCH

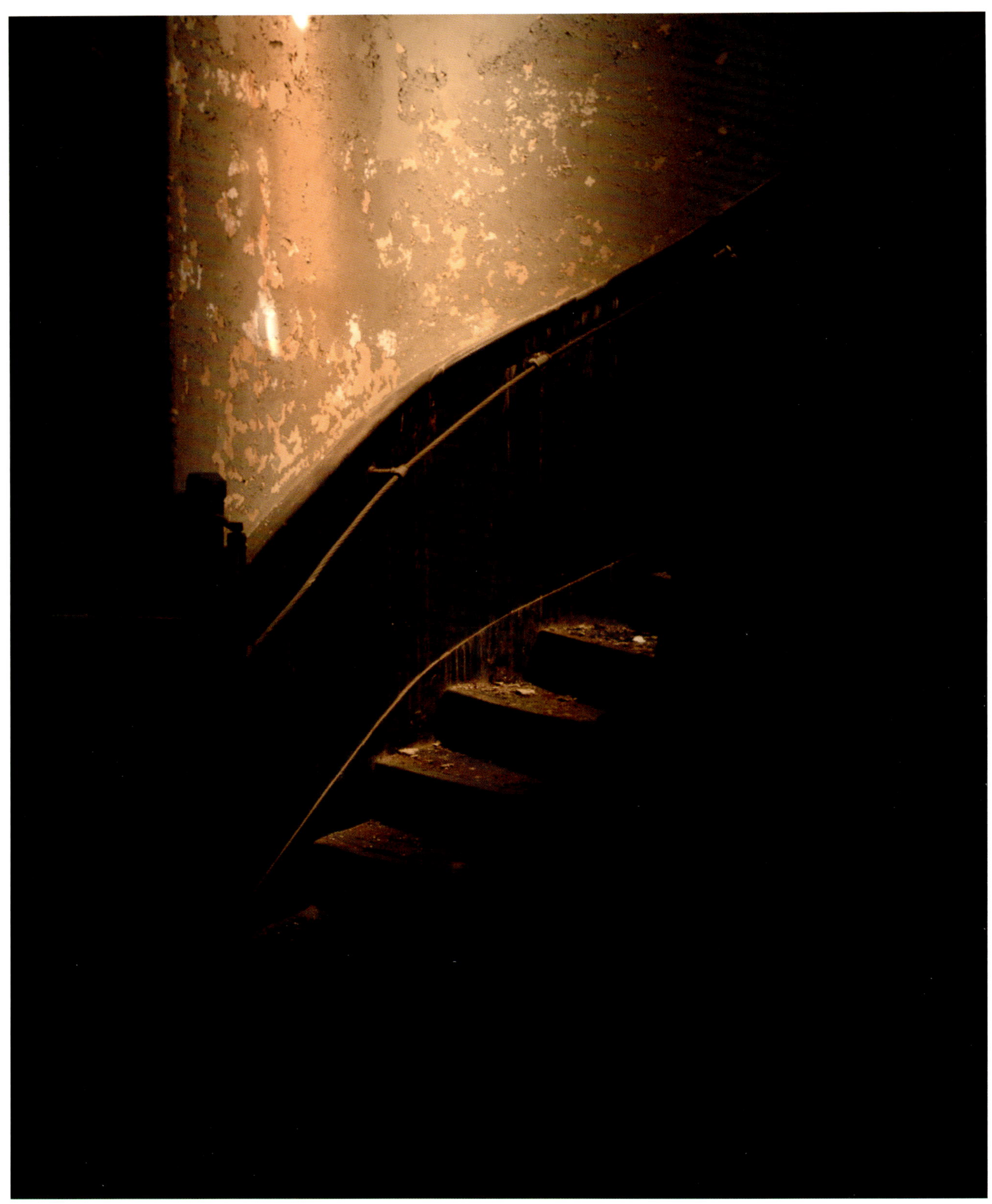

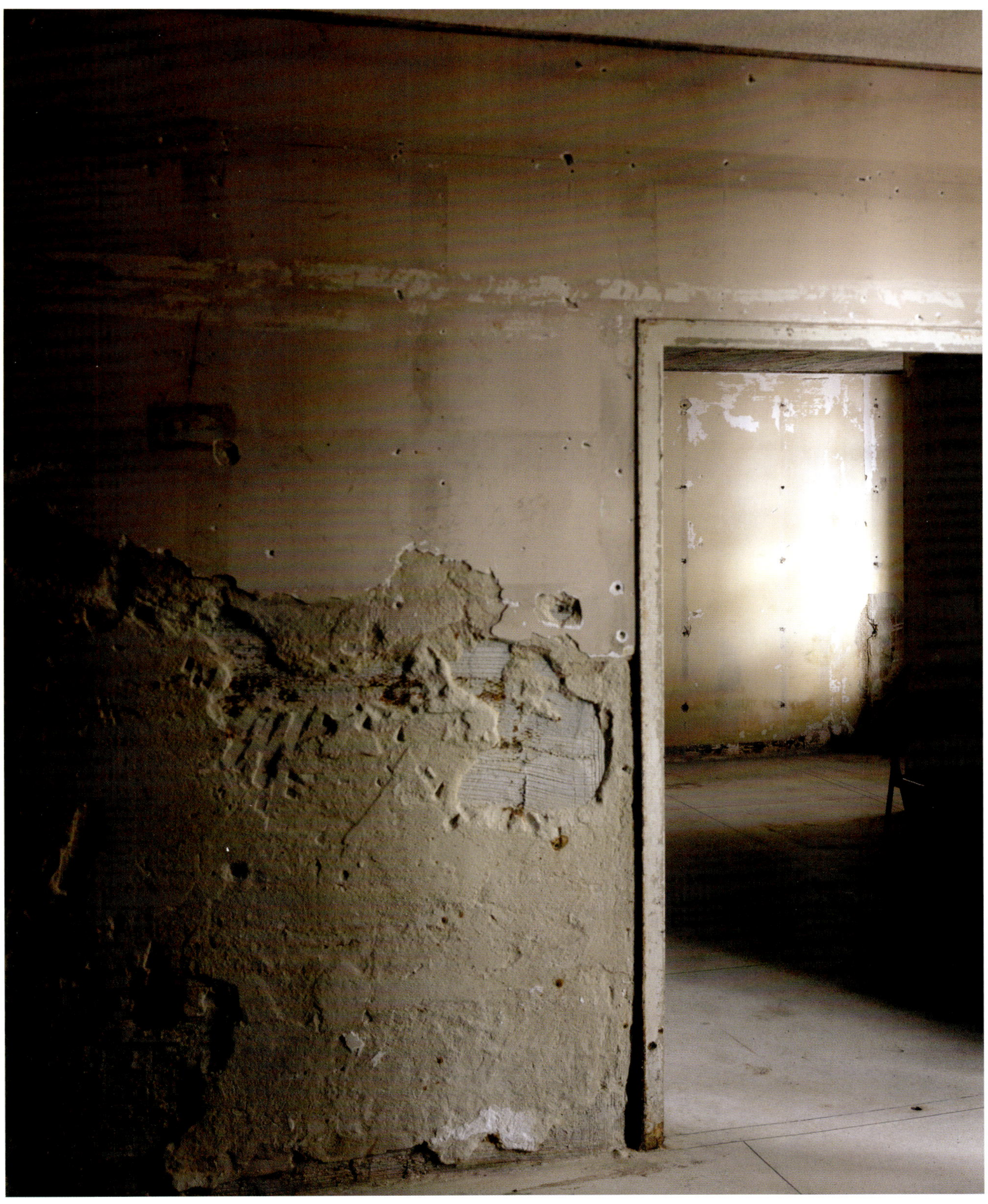

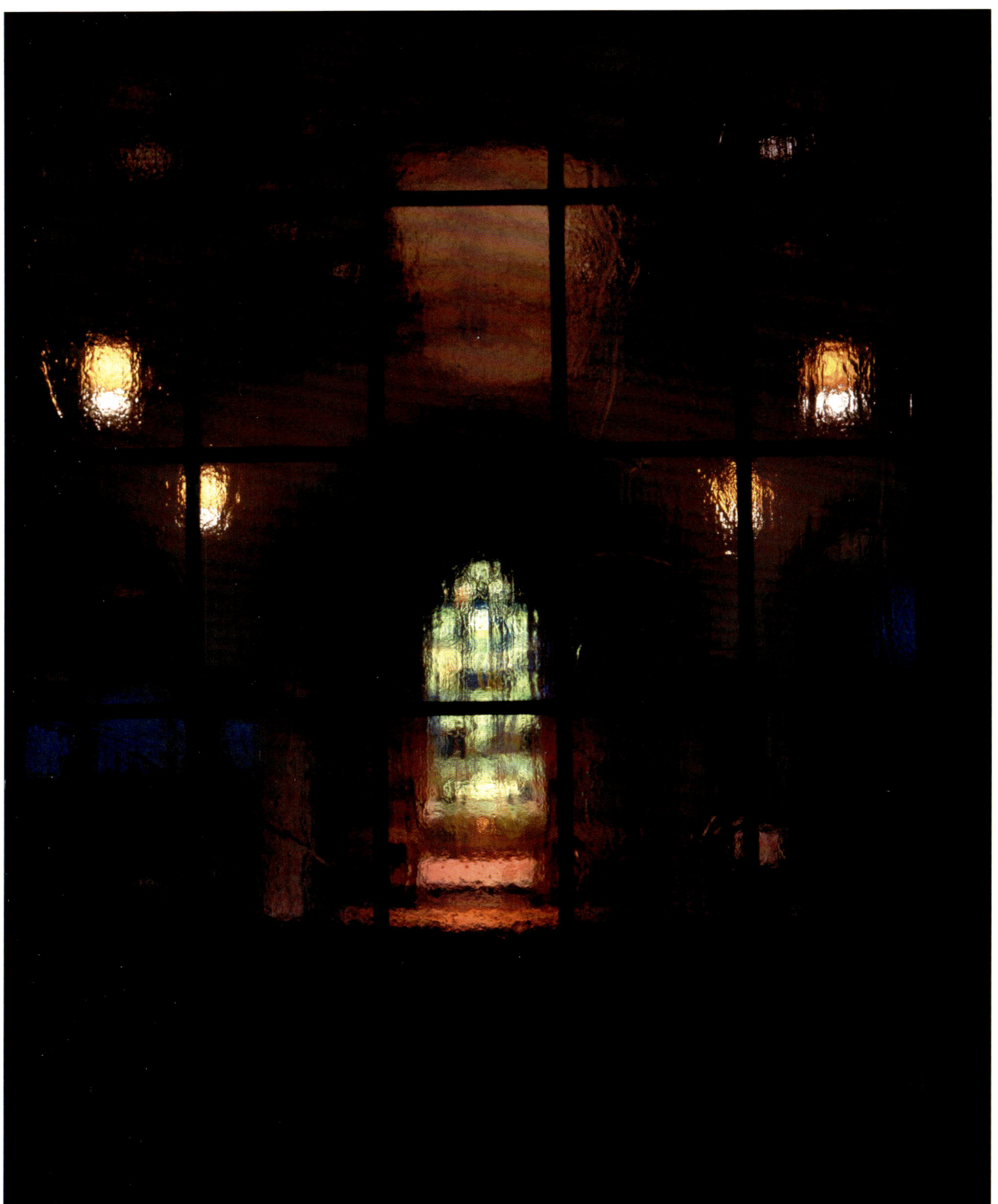

NOTES ON THE WORK

p.ii   *Angel with lamp, Ascension of Our Lord Catholic Church, Donaldsonville, Louisiana.* This is one of the few digitally manipulated pictures. An out-of-focus, distracting stained-glass window behind the angel was removed.

Altars, Chancels, and Sanctuaries

p. 3   *Sanctuary, dancing angels, Our Lady Star of the Sea Catholic Church, New Orleans, Louisiana.* In a church that now has an African American congregation, this chancel of angels done in a blue color scheme represents all the ethnic peoples who at one time used to worship here.

p. 4   *Altar, St. Stephen Catholic Church, New Orleans, Louisiana.* On this day the large stained-glass windows were open, airing out the sanctuary and flooding the altar with natural daylight.

p. 5   *Chancel, Our Lady of Immaculate Conception Catholic Church, New Orleans, Louisiana.*

p. 6   *Sanctuary, Corpus Christi Catholic Church, New Orleans, Louisiana.*

p. 7   *Altar, Most Holy Name of Jesus Church, on Loyola University campus, New Orleans, Louisiana.* I accidentally set off a hidden alarm located in the chancel area.

p. 8   *Sanctuary, Our Lady of the Holy Rosary Catholic Church, New Orleans, Louisiana.* The natural daylight comes from a skylight.

p. 9   *Sanctuary, Our Lady of Lourdes Catholic Church, New Orleans, Louisiana.*

p. 10   *Altar, Christ Church Episcopal Cathedral, New Orleans, Louisiana.* Paintings below the altar are representative of the four gospels: St. Matthew, symbolized by a man; St. Mark, symbolized by a lion; St. Luke, symbolized by an ox; and St. John, symbolized by an eagle.

p. 11   *Chapel sanctuary, Christ Church Episcopal Cathedral, New Orleans, Louisiana.*

p. 12   *Sanctuary, St. Mary's Catholic Church, Old Ursuline Convent, New Orleans, Louisiana.* As was the custom of the times, the place of the host called the monstrance was made from encrusted precious donated jewels collected from the congregation.

p. 13   *Sanctuary, St. John the Baptist Catholic Church, New Orleans, Louisiana.* This well-known landmark church with gold onion top spires can plainly be seen from I-10 crossing St. Charles Avenue.

p. 14   *Altar, Holy Trinity Greek Orthodox Cathedral, New Orleans, Louisiana.* Holy of Holies, only the priest is allowed behind the screen. The icon painting of Madonna and child are seen to the left of the altar screen.

p. 15   *Sanctuary, St. Patrick Catholic Church, New Orleans, Louisiana.* The magnificent dome was lit by natural daylight from skylights in a hidden room and from the roof above the dome.

p. 16   *Chapel, Academy of the Sacred Heart, New Orleans, Louisiana.*

p. 17   *Altar, Saint Maurice Catholic Church, New Orleans, Louisiana.*

p. 18   *Chapel, Notre Dame Seminary, New Orleans, Louisiana.* The first time I tried to photograph this altar, a seminary student was practicing his homily. I came back another day.

p. 19   *Sanctuary, Sacred Heart of Jesus Catholic Church, New Orleans, Louisiana.*

p. 20   *Sanctuary, The Saint Louis Catholic Cathedral, New Orleans, Louisiana.* This cathedral is normally full of tourists and worshipers; I was lucky this day to find it quiet, empty of people, and the altar lit with natural daylight.

Angels, Deities, Madonnas, and Saints

Light